The Darkest Years

— A Famine Story

The Darkest Years

— A Famine Story

Michael Mullen

Cavendish House Publications

Cover Picture: Frank Dolan, Westport, Co. Mayo

Printers: Connaught Telegraph, Castlebar, Co. Mayo, Ireland

This book is dedicated to the nameless victims of The Great Famine.

MAYO : BARONIES
TIRERAGH
ERRIS
TIRAWLEY
SLIGO
GALLEN
BURRISHOOLE
CARRA
COSTELLO
CLARE ISLAND
MAYO
ROSCOMMON
MURRISK
CLANMORRIS
ROSS
KILMAINE
GALWAY

1845: FIRST WARNINGS

THERE was little inkling in the opening months of 1845 that there was any danger of future hunger and death. The potential danger was obvious, the implications alarming.

As Cecil Woodham-Smith writes.

"In the eighteen-forties, after nearly seven hundred years of English domination, Irish poverty and Irish misery appalled the traveller. The Frenchman de Beaumont found in Ireland the extreme of human misery, worse than the Negro in his chains; the German traveller Kohl wrote that no mode of life in Europe could seem pitiable after one had seen Ireland."

The population of Mayo had surged forward since the end of the eighteenth century, the marginal lands were now in cultivation and men had moved on to the flanks of the mountains, seeking space to plant the potato. There was too much reliance on the potato, particularly the lumper, and a failure of this crop could spell death.

In the opening months of 1845 there is much international news to occupy the readers both of the *Connaught Telegraph* and the *Mayo Constitution*, a rival paper in the town. There is much writing concerning the railways, Maynooth College, the Corn Laws, **Daniel O Connell** and

Queen Victoria, still almost a girl. Local news is hard to find. It is usually consigned to the small corners or on show in the reports of the Petty Sessions.

Frederick Cavendish berates the town for the condition of the streets.

"We have so frequently directed public attention to the disgracefully filthy state in which the town is embedded from the accumulation of mire which has been culpably allowed to overspread the public roads and foot-paths, that we now, for curiosity sake, ask if there be any person vested with authority to have the streets and lanes cleaned."

The petty sessions of January deal with trouble in Linenhall Street, Castlebar, on a fair day. A policeman was injured and the judge remarked that the offence demanded the punishment of transportation.

A time will come in 1847 when starving people will plea to be transported.

In April the death of **Augustus Moore** is recorded. It occurred in Liverpool where he fell from a horse called 'Micky Free'. The ground had hardened and Augustus was carried off to hospital where he died. **George Henry**, who had remained in Ireland, was walking on the afternoon of the race, down the avenue of Moore Hall with a cousin; both caught sight of a figure near the gate, seemingly that of Augustus.

It is said that Augustus would have made an outstanding mathematician. He was buried in the family vault beside the lake, celebrated later by his nephew George Moore.

There are lighter moments at the Petty Sessions where all life, as then lived, is exposed.

"A woman name Kelly, from the neighbourhood of Breaffy, charged a respectable looking female, with the seduction of her goose, through the criminal agency of a gander which she kept for that purpose."

Of course to read the case further is to realise that the old woman is speaking broken English and many phrases are Irish. She is entertainment for the gentry and the middle-class. She is a character much beloved of the Anglo Irish and celebrated in Anglo-Irish literature. Here we have an attitude towards the Irish language and those who spoke Irish; humorous and feckless. They would be the weakest and most remote. Their deaths would go unrecorded.

We have good descriptions of the town prior to the famine.

This is what Inglis has to say in 1834:

"Castlebar is not so pretty a town as Westport; but it is a place of greater business.There is only one good street in Castlebar; but the town contains many lanes; and has very long bad suburbs of mud cabins...I found great want of employment in Castlebar. There had recently been a considerable demand for labour on public works, - a new gaol, and new barracks, having been lately constructed....I could purchase at Castlebar, as much potheen as I had a mind, at 3s. 4d the gallon."

Barrow writes in 1835.

"Castlebar is a pretty town of one street, which runs up the gently sloping side of a hill, with narrow

cross streets on each side; the houses good and evidently inhabited by a respectable class of merchants and shop keepers.....it is an improving town; the population in 1831 was 6,373. There is a linen-hall at Castlebar, but it was said that there was "nothing doing " at this time. Just outside the town stands a very handsome jail, the finest building of its sort I have hitherto seen in Ireland. The town seemed, as is usually the case, to abound with beggars..."

At some distance from the town on the road towards Pontoon stood the Workhouse, a formidable and well constructed building.

And in April there is the discovery of Illicit Distillations of poteen in Turlough. **Lieutenant E. B. Browne,** after a march of twelve miles with his men, seized in the Parish of Turlough two stills, two heads and two worms and destroyed a large quantity of potale and singlings. Later in the week they again raided the parish and confiscate more property and several gallons of illicit spirit.

In July there were bonfires in Breaffy to celebrate the birthday of the heir to the estate ... a musician was in attendance, which enabled the rustic lads and lasses, all attired in their holyday dresses, to trip it gaily on the light fantastic toe, while the cheers of the multitude, proclaimed their love and attachment of the gallant Colonel and his family..

On Thursday two factions, who had quarrelled at the fair of Aughagower, agreed to have a fight at the market of Westport. The police arrived and the two factions joined against them. The reporter remarks.

"I have been twenty years in Westport and never witnessed anything to equal the excitement; several people were seriously cut and bruised, but many lives must have been lost were it not for the timely arrival of Captain Higgins, who remained on horseback, parading the streets until past 10 o'clock."

But away from the town people lived in the poorest conditions. Their houses were one-roomed, windowless mud cabins. In some cases pigs slept with their owners and manure heaps choked the doors. The land lord could evict people at will. There would be many evictions during the continuing famine.

However in June of 45 the Connaught reports that the potato crop was prospering. At the Fair of Ballyhean black cattle were in good demand.

At the Petty Sessions **Judy Moran** summoned **John** and **Mary Jordan**, for an assault and for impounding her cow in the defendant's house. Being sworn, she stated that she went and demanded the cow, and for doing so **John Jordan** beat her with a stick and his wife pelted her with stones.

An Achill man writes to the Constitution pleading that harbours should be build at Achillbeg, Keel and Keem. His letter was well written and persuasive. There had been many disasters in Achill on account of the lack of harbours.

June slips into August in the town. It is during this month that disease is noted amongst the potato crop on the Isle of Wight. This was the "blight". It had already ravaged the potatoes in North America. Now England lay exposed and the Government sensed danger. The English worker had become reliant on the potato during the Napoleonic wars. By mid-August the blight had moved into Kent.

Life continued as normal in Castlebar. In Castlebar Workhouse the following articles were ordered during the month. 170lbs of bread;110 stone of potatoes;136 lbs of meal; 290 quarts of milk; 30 boxes of turf; 16 lbs of beef; 7 lbs of chops; half a ton of straw.

There were 84 inmates in the Workhouse.

The markets and fairs bring in good reports and the potato crop shows promise.

Then in September 9th the arrival of the potato blight in Ireland is reported in the *Dublin Evening Post.*

The danger is drawing closer to County Mayo and in September 16 we read:

"In regard to potatoes, we fear that the disease now so much spoke of, prevails to a considerable extent although much more limited than in England, as far as yet been ascertained. But a month must yet elapse before the general digging of potatoes will enable the farmer to estimate the damage. The accounts are very conflicting."

The *Connaught Telegraph* in its September issue speaks of The Potato Cholera and is much more certain of the danger.

"Several persons, residents of Castlebar, have informed us that while digging potatoes in their

fields they encountered an intolerable stench, which after examination, they found to proceed from the putrid state of the esculents they were in the act of unearthing . . .should this fearful malady spread among the crops of the rural population dreadful indeed, must be the consequence to the poor...."

The first dangerous note has been struck. The blight has arrived.

In the same edition, we discover that an infant in a state of nudity was left by its mother in the hall of a house in Castle Street. It would be later taken to the workhouse.

And there was alarm in the town when a man's trousers and shirt were found on the bank of the river near the military barracks. The police were sent for but nobody was found. It was later discovered they belonged to a soldier.

On September 16 **Thomas Davis** dies in Dublin of scarlatina. He was only thirty years of age, yet he had left a considerable body of literature behind him.

In October **Daniel O Connell** visits Castlebar. *The Constitution* downgrades the arrival of the Liberator.

"At about eleven o'clock the trades of Castlebar, each with its banner and accompanied by what was called the temperance band, proceeded to meet Mr. O Connell . . . The place for meeting Mr. O'Connell was French-hill.

The procession arrived in town at about three'o clock, presenting a wretched appearance, from the heavy rains. It proceeded down the Main Street, across which triumphal arches were erected, and by Linen-hall where the meeting was held. It was at first intended to hold it at Flynn's hotel, opposite the church, and the platform was partly erected; but the Earl of Lucan and some other magistrates gave orders that it should be removed, as it would obstruct the public passage if erected there. ... the banquet was given in a pavilion erected at the rear of Flynn's hotel.

The pavilion was tastefully got up, but when the rain began to pour in, as it did plentifully, many wished themselves in a more substantial and waterproof structure. There was a gallery for the ladies behind the chairman's table, and three parallel lines of tables ran from that down the length of the pavilion.

We understand that upwards of four hundred tickets were purchased and the pavilion seemed to be well filled. The prices were, for dinner and wine tickets 8s.6p and for a dinner-ticket alone 4s. 6p.'

This report is interesting as it give one some idea of the paper's attitude and that of Lord Lucan to O'Connell. The *Connaught,* of course, comes out in large columns to celebrate the occasion. So the social structure of the town was solid and events were ordered and well attended.

Late in October the first notes of panic begin to appear.

"We have made enquiries of persons from different parts of this county, relative to the disease which is said to have attacked the potato, but could not learn from any one individual that he had seen it either in his own potatoes or in those of any of his

neighbour........ We are unwilling to contemplate the contrary of this, or to believe that the extent of the disease is such as has been represented, for the consequence would be frightful....."

However at the end of the month the reports on the potato have moved into the centre of the columns and been given hard firm print. The disease cannot be properly defined.

"The disease which now so formally threatens our own country, last year destroyed three fourths of the potato crop of the united states of America, as well as a large proportion of those of France, Germany, Belgium and Holland; and whatever be the mysterious origin of the disease-whether it is to be found in a fly or a fungus, it is but too plain that no effectual remedy has been devised for the disease."

In November there in no longer reasonable doubt. The blight has struck and its first effects are apparent.

"In some cases the people, seeing the destruction of the potatoes in the pits, are leaving them in the ground, in the hope that they will be safer there than if dug and placed in pits or together, and we have heard of some cases where the disease had made such progress that the crop was abandoned altogether, as not worth being dug, or the trouble of attempting to save it........The rumour that the ports would be opened, and the exportation of grain prevented, caused oats to fall in price from the height it had reached owing to the failure in the potato crop...At the meeting of the board of guardians it was resolved that a machine would be

purchased, to grind diseased potatoes and extract the farina from them, for such persons as brought them to the workhouse for that purpose."

The county begins to slide towards famine.

In December we read:

"We have since our last publication heard gentlemen, who are as well qualified as any others in the country to give accurate opinion on the subject, say that the vast number of the people will not have a potato to eat in a month, or six weeks.....This is a frightful prospect."

Despite the famine other news is reported. There was a murderous attack at Milebush by Conway and Prendergast, who lived at Lightford. They made a desperate attach with sticks and stones upon three men belonging to Milebush. So dreadfully where these men beaten that the life of one of them was despaired of, and the others received several dangerous wounds. A woman, the wife of one of the beaten men, who attempted to save her husband, was struck with a stone by one of the savages, and severely cut on the head. The only provocation said to have been given, was that a girl connected with some of the attacking party was offended in some way by the "wren-boys" of Milebush.

Everywhere there are letters and news items which suggest that the potato has failed.

There is talk of public works in Castlebar to provide employment. It recommended that the beds of rivers should be deepened and obstructions on the Moy and the Clydagh removed. The Earl of Lucan is determined to make a cut from Saleen to the river below or at the black quarry, through or near his own farm yard, where a mill might be worked.

It is the year of the beginning of the famine. In these columns the poor have little voice. Most of them spoke Irish and they lived far from the towns. To them the blight was the signature of death put on their brief and hard lives.

Family viewing rotten potatoes, August 1846.

1846: THE FATAL FLAW

IN EARLY January Mr. Bianconi had notified the General Post office that it was his intention to discontinue the running of his cars from Ballina to Belmullet.

In Balla, Rev Mr. Browne, P.P., thanks a Captain Jones who has given him half an acre of land, quite convenient of Belcarra, as an eligible site upon which to erect a chapel.

Hundred of carts, laden with herring from Boffin and the Killeries, are seen passing through Castlebar for the towns of Ballina, Killala, Crossmolina, Foxford, etc.

However, there is not enough salt to keep them fresh.

They have turned black in transit and are now rotting.

But a dark note is sounded concerning the potatoes. Those that have been dug and pitted have been lost and that this will mean hunger for many. *"Fever too, we regret to state, is very prevalent in this town and neighbourhood at present. Alas! what will become of the poor? Famine and disease stalks abroad - the grain has been shipped from our coasts, to fill the granaries of England. Our population are without permanent or remunerative employment and, to crown all, the drivers are impounding for the November rents.*

The word fever will recur again and again so it is necessary to give some definition to the peril. There were two types of fever; typhus and relapsing fever. Typhus ... a common name for three acute infectious diseases of humans caused by rickettsial bodies. Epidemic typhus is caused by the bacillus Rickettsia prowazeki, which is transmitted by the body louse. Symptoms appear about ten days after the victim has been bitten by and infected body louse, and they include high fever, pain in the muscles and joints, stiffness, headache, and cerebral disturbance....

Rickettsia make their way into the human blood-stream through the skin; the bite of the louse is intensely irritating, the victim scratches, the skin is broken, Rickettsia enter and infection takes place....it can also enter as fine dust through the eyes and can be inhaled.

In Irish the word for typhus is black fever.

Relapsing fever is quite different. It occurs where poor nutrition and unhygenic conditions are prevalent. In times of famine the incidence of the disease may reach epidemic proportions.

During the famine they had not been defined or differentiated and they were often confused.

There is no immediate panic in Castlebar and few were interested in definitions. The repsectable inhabitants wished to see extra police drafted into the town.

"Another reason why we look upon the utlity and the necessirty of having policemen stationed at the lower end of the town is that the pig-market is now

held there and the Constabluary at the upper part of the town cannot be supposed to be at all times ready to quell the numerous riots which occur in Staball, Linenhall St., Sruphane, Gallowshill, etc., particularly after night."

Now a wider issue is introduced in the papers. There is a call to have the Corn Laws appealed. These tarriffs on imported grain into England kept the price of English bread high and protected the English farming class. If the Corn Laws were repealed the farming community would be sorely hit. Peel the Prime Minister knew that only the large imports of corn from abroad could relieve a widespread famine in Ireland.

In April the first grim leader is written by Frederick Cavendish:

"The gaunt and long-dreaded scourge has at last broken forth... Even at Turlough, in the immediate neighbourhood of this town, many families are at this moment, we learn, without food- and the wretched sufferers are in vain endeavouring to get provisions on time that their children may not die. At the market of Castlebar, on Saturday last provisions which hitherto were considered reasonable, rose to an alarming height — potatoes from 2 and a half pence to 5d a stone and oatmeal from 13s to 16s per cwt."

Further in April we read of Indian meal being imported in to Mayo:

"It is stated that there can be no fear of starvation while the Government stores are well supplied with Indian Corn, and that several Steamers, freighted by Government, have landed their cargoes of

foreign corn on the quay of Westport. The later part of the statement is true - - provisions have been landed in Westport from war steamers. This supply has not, however, contributed to increase the quantify of provisions in the country - for at the very time the Indian meal was landing, several vessels were receiving on board, for export, cargoes of Irish oats and meal."

In late April it is evident that the famine will continue to makes its fatal progress. Already people see no future in remaining in Castlebar and during this month they begin to move in carts and jaunting cars to Westport in order to emigrate. For the poor in Castlebar it is hoped that they will be given employment in order to fend off hunger.

During April we hear that between the old brewery and the dilapidated shambles there are constantly to be seen dogs floating or stuck in the mud, flung into the water by some ruffians who have no regard for the health of their fellow men.

In the country around Castlebar the farmers have begun to plant potatoes.

And this sad voice of the people is recorded by R. Moor, Rector and Vicar of Cong. He had been visited by the heads of many families who said:

"Sir, we are starving — we have had but one meal a day for some time past — our little seed we are obliged to eat — we can get no work — what are we and our families to do? God knows we would do anything short of death rather than be obliged to commit violence.."

The letter demonstrates that starvation is now extreme. Soon people will begin to die, individually, then it will be in great numbers. The Great Famine is now beginning.

In August it is reported that all the potatoes about Castlebar have failed.

"We regret also to say that a blight has come on the oat crop; in many fields around this town, one third at least has been already rendered useless by smut. During last week a report prevailed that the rooks were all dying in the fields and rookeries. The dew on last Friday night has done immense damage to the growing crops. The potato tops have been nearly all withered away by it and several persons have declared to us that they had put some of this dew on their tongues to try if it were honey; it proved however , very bitter and many found it to emit a disagreeable smell....One thing is certain, the staple food of the people is gone."

It is a time for desperate measures to be taken by the government but no such measure are taken. People plead for work. From all over the county the hunger is turning to starvation. It is a very short step to death.

Even those on relief are not paid and we have this following account:

"It has often been our lot alas! to witness scenes of distress in May, but never can the sights of Friday and Saturday last be effaced from the recollection of the inhabitants of the town. So early as seven o'clock on Friday morning a hundred of those wretched beings - walking skeletons - employed on the public works, crowded our streets in quest of their wages; all declaring "they were ready to fall for want of food; that they had not been paid their

hard earned pittance for the last three weeks; that the gombeen people had stopped their supplies and that they knew not how to act."

The gombeen-man and the middleman are busy providing work and tickets for their own on the public work schemes. They are fiddling the system. During the famine we will find many cases of such corruption.

"It is an insult to the individuals who issue the tickets, and an injury to the poor widows and orphans deprived of bread by factious overseers - who for a glass or two of poteen whiksey turn them off to make room for favourites, that stand in no need of such work."

When a population is weak and ill nourished it is vulnerable to fever and in September fever struck close to Castlebar.

"We regret to state that fever, to an alarming extent, has at length made its appearance in this county. Our Foxford Correspondent states, that never, in his memory, was fever so prevalent in that locality as at present. In the villages, between that town and Pontoon, entire families are lying and many dying. He mentions one family in particular, eight of whom are confined to the bed of sickness, their only attendant being a boy of six years old. Several other families have no person to wet their parched lips, the neighbours being in dread to approach the cabins of contagion."

In October the price of food continues to rise and there is no meal at the government depots in Castlebar, Westport, Killala.

.....How could labourers support eight or nine in

family at 10d per day government money, while the price of meal is 23s per cwt. and the speculators — the blood-sucking, flesh-consuming gombeen Shylocks are already calculating on obtaining thirty shillings per. cwt. in this town. This comes from allowing forestallers to buy up the provisions and again resell them at an enormous profit.

And yet there is nobility to be found.

A man of the village of Barnastang, Glenisland, with a family of six children, himself and wife, in all eight persons, were on Monday morning last in that low degree, from hunger that our informants states "the most of them could not survive until night. With much difficulty the poor man made his way to the house of **Pat Malley**, a neighbour who was is in great want himself, having no provisions but as he buys at the market. "He could not" he said "see his neighbour die while God left him anything" and he forthwith went out, took out one of his four sheep and handed it over to McHugh to kill for himself and family."

In November the fever has spread to Castlebar, Ballyheane Breaffy and Errew, In Castlebar it reached the cabins of the starving poor. And there is no hospital in Castlebar where the fever can be contained.

People begin to die. The inquests are reported from Crossmolina.

Michael Walsh - Verdict. Died from famine.

Martin McGiver - Verdict; died from want of a sufficiency of food.

And so it continues.

December arrives and we read in the issue of

December 16:

"Food is now so dear that it is impossible for the poor to purchase it ... the consequence is the people are dying of hunger, and the Coroners of the county have busy work of it in holding inquests on emaciated bodies. We cannot venture to give even an idea of the suffering around us."

Starvation and death become familiar. The town is crowded with beggars and mendicants. They cry out for food. The town is not only hungry . It is starving.

"On Monday evening a poor man dropped dead in Staball from hunger. The unfortunate creature was buried on the same night without a coffin.... scarcely a day passes that our ears are not saluted with the death knell of some three or four persons being carried for interment. It is not unusual to witness three funerals together in the old church yard. As to the cause of death, the answer is "fever and want."

In this cold month a woman is seen carrying a dead child in her arms through Castlebar begging for money to purchase a coffin.

The terrible year ends.

1847 opens and the leader runs as follows:

"1847. You have us subdued; you have found us crushed down by starvation, disease and death; be it in the happy destiny to change this order of things; to stay the ravages of famine; to throw over the troubled earth the cornucopia to cheer the drooping, bereaved, and the broken hearted.....Buoyed up with this hope we bid thee 1847! a thousand welcomes!

But it did not live up to these expectations.

1847 was to be the worst of years. It was the year which has scarred our memory.

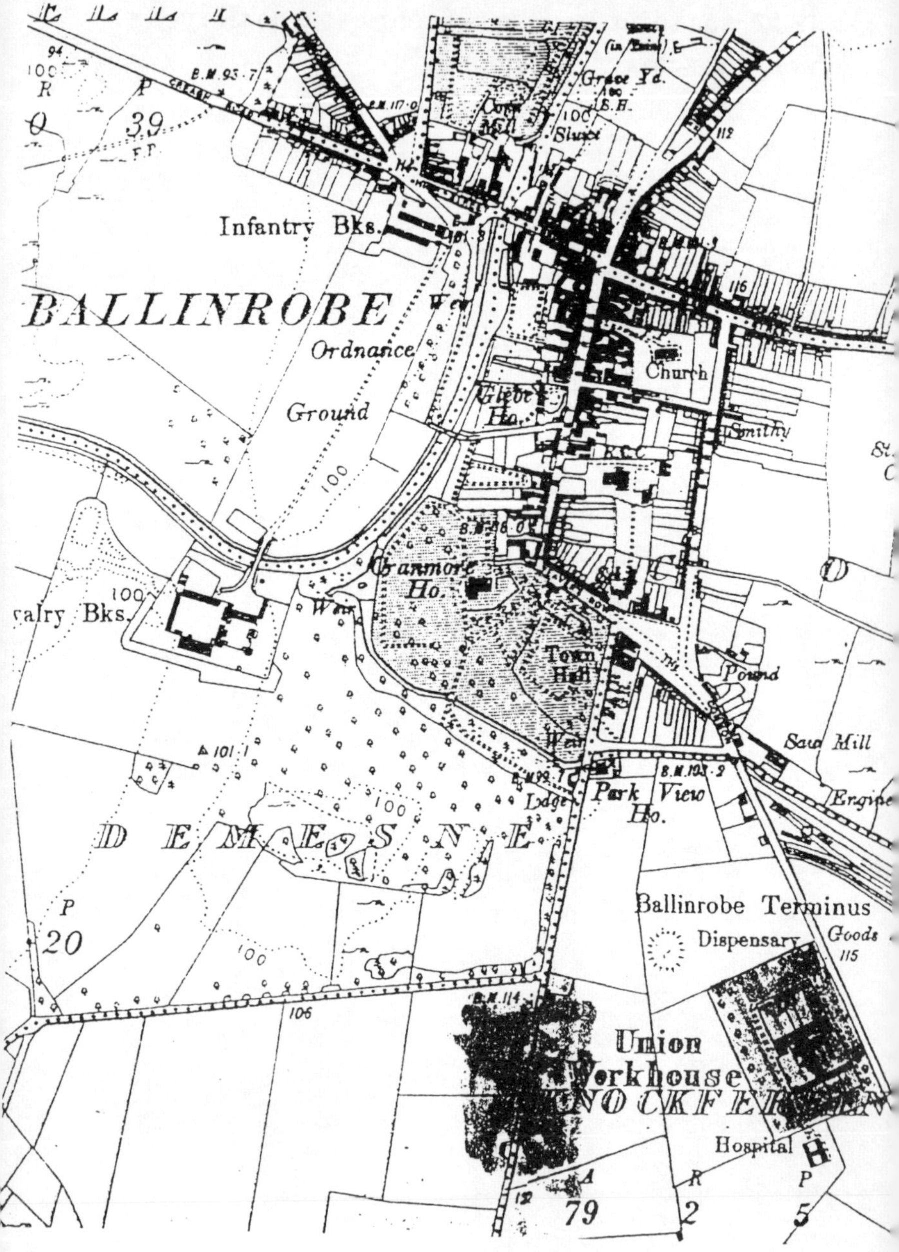
BALLINROBE
Infantry Bks.
Ordnance
Ground
Church
Smithy
Glebe Ho.
Cranmore Ho.
Town Hall
Pound
Saw Mill
Park View Ho.
Lodge
D E M E S N E
Ballinrobe Terminus
Dispensary
Goods
Union Workhouse
Hospital
Grave Yd.
Sluice
Corn Mill
Weir
valry Bks.
39
20
79
2
5

BLACK '47

The year would be called Black '47. It was a year of famine and fever and it would leave a physical and psychological mark on the county. All previous famines prior to this, were accompanied by the fever.

The victim's face swelled up and darkened and that was why it was called the black fever in Irish. It was accompanied by delirium, vomiting and even gangrene and always a terrible stench. This was one of the many illnesses which attended the famine victims.

The number who died from typhus is unknown but it was extremely high. It affected the middle-class as well as the poor and the incidents of death was very high amongst priests and clergymen.

Forty-seven began badly. It was to be a dark year and the gloom would spread into '48

At the beginning of January food was so scarce and expensive in **Castlebar** that a committee was formed from all the persuasions of the parish to purchase food and set up soup kitchens.

It could do little to solve the problem of hunger. The Workhouse which had been built a few years earlier, through mismanagement and incompetence, housed only 130 persons, although it was built to serve 600.

In 1847 on a Friday evening in July 3,000 starving men, women and children would choke all roads leading to the gates as they sought entry.

At an inquest held in the Parish of **Kilmovee** at the beginning of the year the jury returned a verdict that the deceased, John Cusack, met his death on the night of January 5th in a cold wet mud cabin from destitution and hunger.

The report runs: *"I attended a poor man, John Cusack, who died a few hours after of starvation. He lived in the village of* ***Aylesmore****. We had nine deaths within the last few days, most of them, if not all, were the effects of starvation."*

A coffin fund was set up in Castlebar in order *"to prevent the recurrence of the inhuman spectacle we witness of people burying the dead without coffins."*

Everywhere there were distressing sights of people dying for the want of food. In Erris hundreds were dying every week in the most distressing conditions.

A Protestant Minister writes:

"A few days ago I entered a miserable cabin, dug out of bog; a poor woman sat propped against the wall inside; the stench was intolerable, and on my complaining of it the mother pointed to a sort of square bed in the corner; it contained the putrid - the absolutely melted away remains of her eldest son."

Another report says,

"At ***Ballycastle,*** *where I reside, inquests have been held on bodies found on the mountain, by the road side, in a ditch, and in deserted houses, into which the poor famished creatures have crawled to breath*

their last and all the verdicts have been, "died through starvation!". At ***Ballynacue*** *, I am informed, a family was forced, last week, to subsist on a dead ass!"*

The same distressing sights were observed in **Castlebar**. A mother was seen making her way down to her family burial ground in Turlough, a distance of four miles, her dead son bound to her back. At Turlough in February seventeen deaths occurred in one week. In one case a father deprived himself of food in order that his wife and children might live.

Deaths were reported in **Gallows Hill** and **Coarsepark** and all efforts to get coffins for people were fruitless. Many had to be buried coffined in wattles and in unsanctified ground.

A riot took place in the workhouse. The paupers were no longer able to endure the diet of raw meal which was served in small quantities. There was neither heat nor clothing available to them and they turned and attacked the master who fled to a place of safety.

Lists of the dead continued to appear in the *Connaught Telegraph*. At **Breaffy** Michael McNally, Peter Swords and James Gavin died of starvation. Now people began to kill horses and asses and eat their flesh in order to survive.

Between 1815 and the start of the famine almost one million and a half Irish people had left Ireland. They were strong and youthful. Now among those who emigrated were the old and the weak and the fevered. They fled from a land which had let them down and a place where no hope remained.

"From ***Tyrawly*** *the numbers daily migrating is astonishing; whole villages are deserted and houses locked up. We know numerous persons from different parts of this county having freeholds who have disposed of their lands, their growing wheat crops, houses, cattle, nay, their Chapel pews drew their money from the saving banks to go to America."*

With the famine, beggars crowded into **Castlebar** and were seen everywhere. In the churchyards the graves made by the paupers from the workhouse are only two feet deep. In another instance close to **Louisburgh** an exposed corpse was found eaten by dogs in a graveyard.

In April we read the following:

"In the ***Westport Union****, the test of outdoor relief has been put into operation, where no less than 30,000 human beings are now receiving gratuitous relief, at a weekly outlay of 1,000 pounds! Thus, while the poor of Westport, are fed and cared for, those in and around* ***Castlebar,*** *are left to die, and after death to be buried without coffins. What a curse hangs over our town and its poor mendicants. On Wednesday last the body of a poor woman was found dead in a field adjoining this town. A child belonging to the deceased had piled some stones round the body to protect it from the dogs and pigs. During the last week several dead bodies were carried through the town for interment without the luxury of coffins."*

In February a beggar was admitted to the **Ballinrobe** workhouse. Some days later he died of typhus. An epidemic broke out and swept through the building. Several people died including some of the staff. In May the fever is also present in **Castlebar** as well as famine. There is a plea to inter the bodies in the graveyards instead of heaping earth upon them. And in May the levelling process begins.

Lord Lucan's crowbar brigade were out and about. They moved to **Gallow's Hill** in Castlebar and threw the cottier occupants onto the road. They had to make their night shelters in ditches and drains. Nature and the landlord was working against them. As the cost of the famine and the Poor Law began to make inroads into the purse of the landlords, they immediately began to evicts the tenants as they were responsible for their rates.

A Poor Law inspector in **County Clare** was to write later . . .*"there were days in that western county when I came back from some scene of eviction so maddened by the sights of hunger and misery I had seen in the day's work that I felt disposed to take the gun from behind my door and shoot the first landlord I met."*

The merchants seized the opportunity to push up the prices of food and soon it became impossible for shopkeepers and ordinary people to purchase food.

The Evangelical Society in the town subsidised cheap food in order to keep people alive. And now to make matters worse, hundreds who were on relief work were struck off and thrown on the charity of others. People no longer bothered to dig the graves to any great depth. Two feet was regarded as sufficient.

The summer came and brought with it the fever. The poor, dressed in filthy rages, carried the fever into the town. One could never get away from the poverty and hunger. The menicants were everywhere, sleeping where they could, crying out each morning for food. However, the potato crop looked strong and healthy around the town and there was no sign of blight.

And the fever took the very best; those who gave spiritual and medical comfort to the poor. Their names deserved to be remembered.

Rev. Francis Kinkead, beloved by the Roman Catholics as he was by the Protestants, whose minister he was.

The **Rev. James Mc Manus** P.P of **Turlough.** Fever, caught in the discharge of his duty in the County Jail; **Rev. Patrick Poundeu**, Protestant Rector of **Westport**; The **Rev. Robert Potter** of **Louisburgh**.

"Of all men living we believe Mr. Potter had no enemy. Fever of a malignant type has now made his large and young family double orphans."

Doctor Hamilton of **Ballinrobe**. Fever contracted while attending in the union workhouse.

Doctor Devlin of **Ballina**.

Doctor Jordan of **Castlebar** the efficient and skilful medical officer of the **Bohola** and **Kiltimagh** Dispensary.

Miss M.A Smith, one of the Sisters of Mercy, who died of the fever, taken from the poor to whose wants she was a ministering angel.

On June 2nd it was announced that the great chieftain **Daniel O'Connell** had died.

'He breathed his last in a foreign land. The peaceful murmurs of the Adriatic sung his dirge and requiem.'

The *'Connaught'* went to press, column and page edged in black.

The weather continued fine and the harvest was promising. The merchants held their food prices high but it was hoped by people that a good harvest would make them tumble.

In July there was some fear that brown spots dotting the leaves might be the beginning of the blight but this fear soon passed. Reports from the country in general were good.

July was the time for elections to The House of Commons. **John Denise Brown**, visited **Islandeady** and met the freeholders. He was accompanied by **Rev. Mr. Henry**, P.P. who spoke for him in Irish.

The August weather was favourable for the crops but helped the spread of the fever. **Rev. William Stoney** set up a temporary hospital in **Gallows Hill** where he had twelve beds prepared. It did little to contain the epidemic which spread down through the streets. People died from the common fever, typhus and scarlet fever.

In June the weather improved for the better and the fever has lessened. But reports continue to pour into the *Telegraph*. We do not know the names of those who died. They would fill too many columns and in many cases their deaths were not reported. One can only take some of the reports and print them.

"From ***Erris*** *the accounts are most dreadful, and*

should the fever and other diseases now raging there continue as at present, we much fear there will not be sufficient left to gather in the scanty crops which some of the inhabitants had put in the ground.

"We have talked to a trusty man in the neighbourhood who told us it is not unusual to see in some villages from ten to twenty dead in a day; that he himself saw the cabins pulled down to cover the remains of a family of six or seven dead inside and that the dead bodies of many persons have been buried in cabbage plots and beside hedges without coffins."

Swinford — Fever still prevalent, but not altogether as virulent in its character as it was some weeks since. Many, are however, dying in and about the town.

Foxford — fever and dysentery have not abated and many are dying in the town and country around from those grievous maladies.

Louisburgh — This town, and the country westward to the **Killeries,** is one charnel emporium of disease; and the number of deaths in the villages along the sea coast is incredible.

It becomes a long and sad litany which will continue week by week

There is some hope expressed for the crops in the July edition of the papers. The potato tops are blooming and the crop seems to give good promise. But then some leaves are dotted with brown spots and crumble to dust when handled.

Emigration continues from the blighted land. The following report occurs in the *Telegraph* in

June:

"In our present publication will be found an advertisement from ***Mr. Flanagan****, Ship Agent,* ***Newport****, announcing that the splendid Ship "Argyle" has been chartered by him to convey passengers from Innisgoula to Quebec. This is a very favourable opportunity for Mayo emigrants and one they should immediately avail themselves of, as by doing so much expense to themselves can be spared. The "Argyle" is expected this day at the harbour of Innisgoula, between Newport and Westport, and is most elegantly fitted up for cabin and steerage passengers."*

In the same month there was a plea to open a burial ground in the Castlebar Workhouse. Each day bodies from the workhouse were carried through the town. The bearers rested the bodies in the Main Street out of sheer exhaustion. New grounds in the workhouse are consecrated as burial places. The journey from the death bed to the grave has been considerably shortened.

In late August fever returns to the town.

In **Shambles Lane** several people are dying. In one house fourteen people lie unattended.

In **Sruphane Street** we read *"In one Lazer house with this dreadful epidemic, so much so that pedestrians going the way can distinctly hear the raving of the unfortunate creatures lying in low dirty hovels".*

Gallows Hill — "This classic region is in a fearful state from fever, and no wonder, for its sooty cabins, beneath the roofs of which a reasonable-sized man could not stand erect, gives shelter at night to a numerous staff of filthy mendicants, who prowl through the town in day time, scattering the fever raging in those piggeries, from house to house; and thus the disease has become general."

Stabball — "Along the whole of this unwholesome and filthy street, fever of every hue - common-typhus - scarlet - rages with the fury of a conquering and invading army. We may be told we are romancing - be it so, facts will bear us out. For the last week, there has been lying in the open street, between **Stabball** and **Richard Street**, a poor woman in fever - her bed the cold earth - her pillow a head of stones - her covering a filthy piece of sheeting.

September 15th brought a harsh editorial aimed at the merchants:

"*You had a jubilee for the last 18 months, while those wretched creatures, scarce able to move, were seen crawling forth, carrying the dead bodies of husband and wife and child without coffin for internment. While you were amassing riches how many of your poor countrymen were buried in their own cabbage plots, or whole families interred in their own cabins by tumbling their roof in on them.*'

At night there were outrages in the town. The shebeens were busy dealing out poteen. The two police stations, one at **Spencer Street** the other at **Newtown** could not cope with the trouble. Every street had it's illicit distillers.

Then in October when the farmers were harvesting their crops, the agents of the landlords moved into the fields and took the grain for rent.

There was anger at the move and night-brigades marched through the countryside but they were ineffective against the agents. The potato crop did not fail and the market on Saturday, October 2nd, was well supplied with potatoes which sold at 4 ½d. to 5d. a stone.

In the same months there were acts of piracy in **Blacksod Bay**. The '*Kate Thorn*,' a sailing ship on it's way to **Newport** from Liverpool was surrounded by ten boats off **Eagle Island**. A wind blew up and it escaped. Not so the '*Elizabeth*' and '*Mary*.' Boarded by banditti of seventy men, they took away about 70 tons of cargo.

There were complaints from the governor of the jail that it was overcrowded. People who had been ejected from their homes were brought up for stealing, charged and sent to prison. In fact people deliberately committed crimes in order to be convicted. Good substantial food was doled out in jail, far better in fact than the food doled out in the Workhouse.

On Christmas morning the Catholic soldiers belonging to the 19th depot marched through the town and attended Mass in the town chapel, armed with their fire locks, pouches and swords. People objected to them leaning on the muzzles of their locks in the church during the Mass.

At the end of December the editor takes leave of a very bleak year:

"In '46 people were killed in hundreds. In '47 they were mowed down in thousands. In '46 they got Christian sepulchre but in '47 they were thrown into holes dug in cabbage gardens, in fields without

coffins. And we have seen the dead carried about in the arms of females begging from door to door."

So it was the town passed through the worst year in its history. It was a year without light and there seemed little light ahead. Those who were not carried off by starvation were visited by the fevers. The tenants were driven from their lands for economic reasons. Their homes and fields would be levelled to make sheep ranches. It was the year when many emigrated.

In the end words fail to describe what happened.

The year was called Black Forty Seven.

But the people were not at the end of their tribulations.

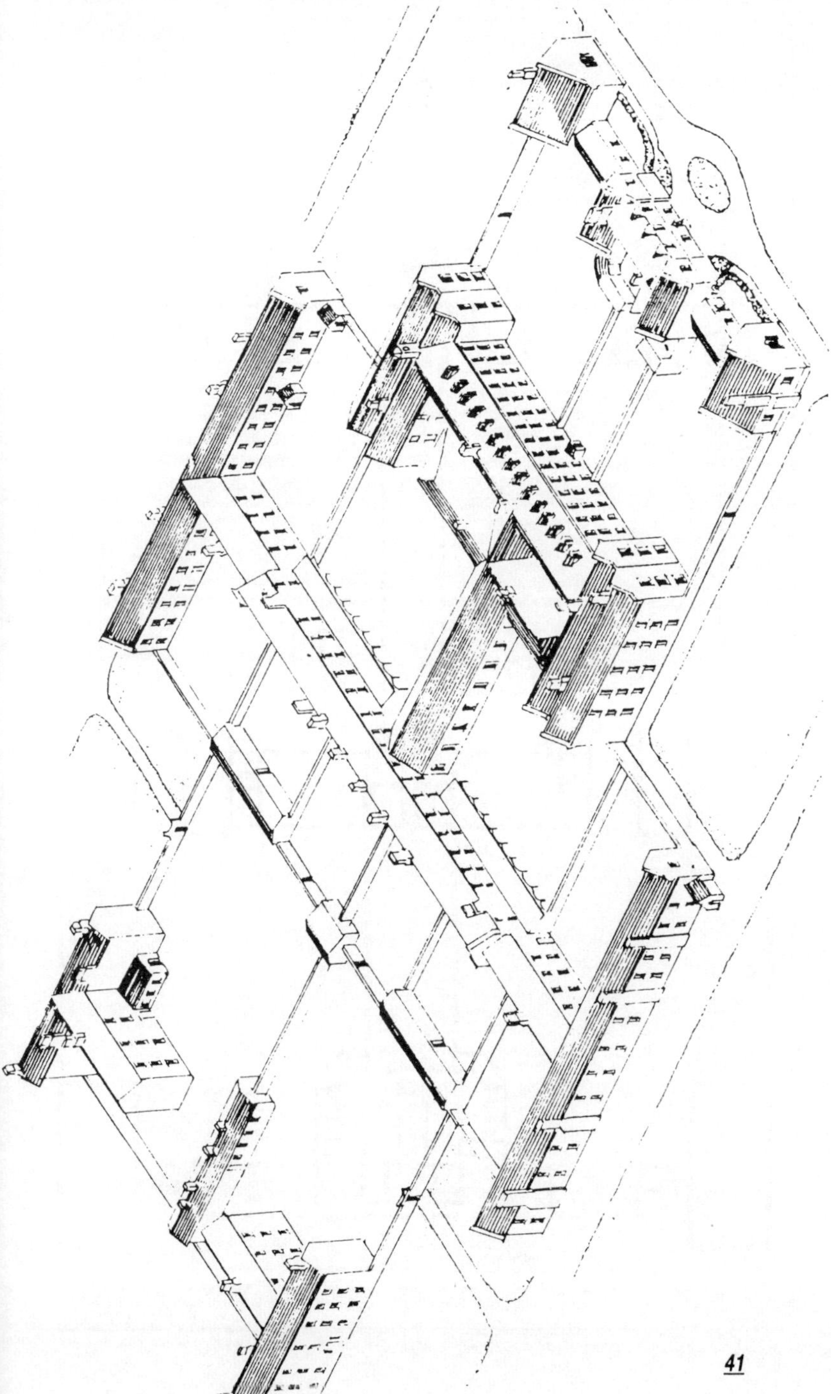

UNION WORKHOUSES, IRELAND.

PLAN

Exhibiting the mode of Enlargement by the erection of Buildings for the Children

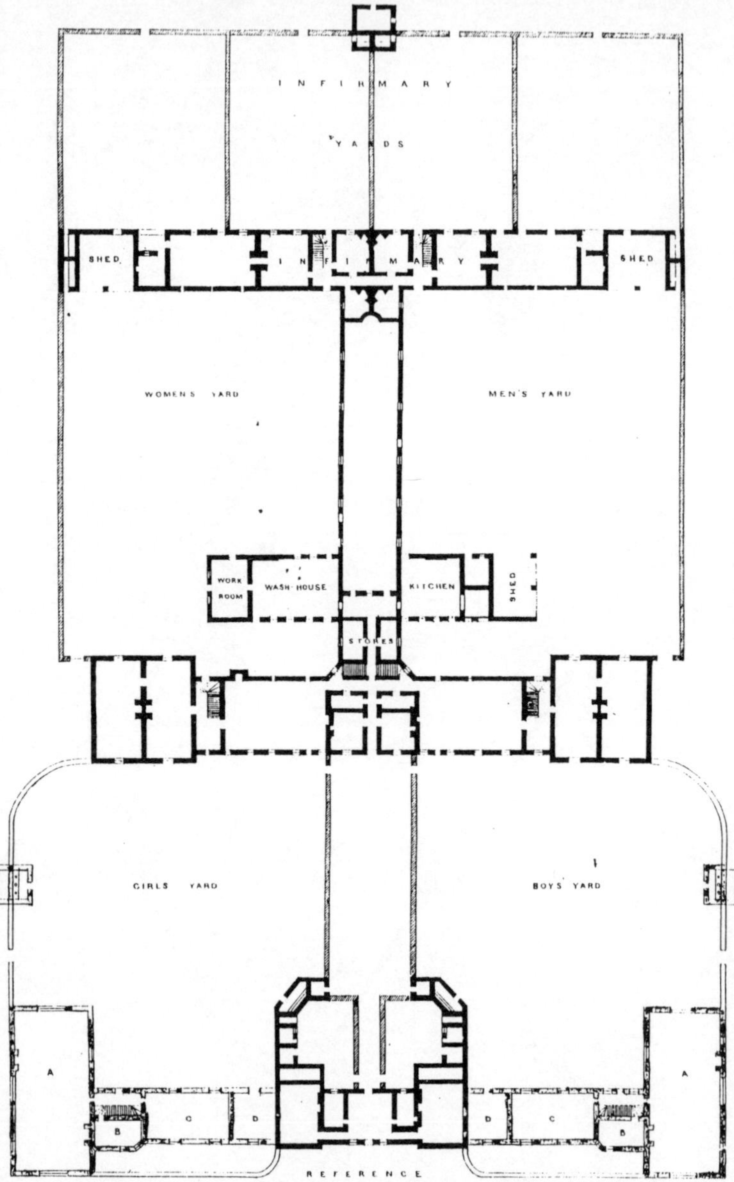

REFERENCE

Present Buildings, colored Blue A A *Boys and Girls School Rooms* — C C *Work Rooms*

Projected Buildings, colored Red B B *School Masters and School Mistresses Rooms.* D D *Washing Places.*

Holbrooke's lithog 2 Crow St Dublin

GEO WILKINSON ARCH[t]

Appendix to First Annual Report of Commissioners of Irish Poor Laws: — App A No 17 (1)

1848.....YEAR OF DARKNESS

Hunger did not cause the royal family any undue worry as they sat down to dinner on Christmas Night. The royal table was laden with a magnificent display of viands both recherche and substantial. The baron of beef was there in all its glory; as well as the boar's head crested with thyme and rosemary. The sideboards were surmounted with stately Christmas trees.

In January there were 782 in the Castlebar workhouse. Thirty three were suffering from fever and seventy eight were suffering from other diseases. The average cost to keep a pauper per week was one shilling and six and a quarter pence.

The potato crop of 1847 had not been affected by blight. The weather was dry but the yield was insufficient. In 1848 the acreage of potatoes would be three times more than in the year previously.

Death from starvation continued. They come as horrific pen pictures, short and fierce in their description:

"John Kean of the electoral Division of Drum, ***Castlebar*** *Union, recently discharged from the Workhouse and put on the outdoor list, died last week from cold and debility. So great was the privation of his neighbours that they could not procure a coffin for him and on Sunday night he*

was buried, tied up in a bundle of wheaten straw! "

While the poor died somebody wrenched off all the knockers on the doors of **Westport**. Even the Sisters of Mercy did not escape the vandalism.

The life in **Castlebar** was confused. As always the poor and the hungry crowded into the towns and the population swelled.

Some of the relief officers were corrupt. They showed favouritism to their cronies while deserving people were cut off from food. Thus they presided over life and death.

"Why has poor Sullivan's family in the center of the town, been allowed to starve while those persons now cut off (the out door relief scheme) were supplied. Was not one of the clergymen of **Castlebar**, on Tuesday last called upon to give the rights of his church to one of the Sullivan's family, who was dying of starvation."

It is impossible to record all the deaths. Sometimes they are set out as stark items.

No.1 — a poor woman found dead on the **Westport Road**, left for days unburied on the side of the road with a stone at the head and another at the feet. A shocking sight!

No.4. — Rose Hoban, of **Knocksaxon**, parish of Strade: eight days dead before she was interred.

No.11. — **Mrs. Kilboyne of Srumphane, Castlebar**, dysentery occasioned by want.

No. 16 — A boy on the **Newport Road**, so long dead that we are told the body had partly melted away.

All about the cemetery the hungry dogs howl at night time.

To cope with the paupers in the town an extra poorhouse was opened at**James Foy's** delapidated hotel, much to the annoyance of **Frederick Cavendish,** the proprietor of the *Connaught Telegraph*:

"*We are again constrained to call attention to the odious end of blasphemous swearing of the youthful paupers next door to our establishment.*"

Poorhouse tickets were issued to those who were supposed to be in dire need. However, these tickets were abused by the relieving officers. Many of the officers, selected to extend the out of door relief were both worthless and corrupt.

Favourites who had houses, lands, milk and butter (luxuries which many ratepayers could not boast of) received relief. No only was this in evidence but in **Corofin** there were reported to be a case where a comfortable farmer was left on the lists, while his neighbour, with nothing in the world but his spade and his limbs, had been struck off.

In February the government gave up the hope of relief works and brought in the "Act for the Temporary Relief of Destitute Persons in Ireland,"

No. 6 — **Peggy Moran**, found dead on the 20th by the ditch side. She applied three times for relief. The third time her name was put on; but she was a corpse when the relief was obtained."

In April we have the following description of conditions in **Stabball:**

*"On Thursday last a poor girl from **Stabball**, named **Regan**, while waiting for relief at the food store, dropped from exhaustion on the street, and*

was carried home apparently lifeless. ***John Carter Barrett, Esq****. Medical Superintendent Carra Dispensary hastened to her miserable abode and by administering restorative stimulants succeeded in producing animation. Having accompanied the Doctor in his work of mercy, we had the opportunity of viewing the domicile of this child of misfortune; the scene of misery which presented itself to our gaze will not soon be forgotten.*

"The hovel, filled with smoke, was about 8 feet by 6; the roof from the floor in or about 7 feet. The poor girl lay stretched on the cold and damp floor; and upon the doctor asking 'why she was not laid on a bed'? the poor and emaciated mother replied: 'Doctor dear, we have no bed; and we did not eat a bit for two days; and it is the hunger that has killed her'. Upon inquiry we ascertained that three other families live in this miserable habitation.

There follows an item on cannibalism in Galway. It is a subject one has no wish to pursue.

The tradesmen of the town pawned their goods at the pawn office in Main Street, while many farmers sold their relief meal ticket and bought sugar and tea.

The well-heeled take advantage of the food tickets. This abuse was highlighted at a court cast held in **Castlebar** earlier where the plaintiff brought a case against a small cottier who had stolen one of his sheep.

In the course of the hearing it turned out that the plaintiff possessed 70 acres of land, sixty sheep, several cattle and barns filled with hay and barley.

In addition he was receiving poor relief on several occasions. In desperation the poor man had stolen the sheep and was discovered by the plaintiff eating it with his family, raw.

For this offence and taking into account the circumstances he received a prison sentence of one year. During the same month at the **Castlebar** Quarter Sessions **James McDonagh**, **John Guinness** and **John Diver**, were transported for seven years for stealing sheep.

Death by starvation continued during the months. While paupers carried their dead through the town from the Workhouse a gullet was being cut between Saleen and Lake Lanack. Fear spread through the town, as it was thought that the river could not take the water and the lower part of the town would be subjected to flooding.

March was the season for emigrating to America. Every Saturday small farmers sold their furniture in the Market Place to buy tickets.

And all the while **Frederick Cavendish** was annoyed by the carry-on in **Foy's Hotel** which he now called 'The Bastille.' The windows were smashed, the contents of chamber pots dashed on the road and handsome young women were doing their business on the top storey.

There was plenty of activity in the Barracks in preparation for St. Patrick's Day. It was feared that there would be trouble in the town. Each soldier was issued with 90 rounds of lead. They were on the alert all day but nothing much happened. In the evening the town was illuminated and blazing barrels of tar were brought through the streets. A 'Castle Roundhead' was discovered in the crowd trying to stir up trouble.

At the end of March the farmers were advised to sow potatoes, turnips, parsnips and carrots and to abandon the grazing crops which had been seized as rent the year previously.

At the beginning of April the pawn shop of **Mr. William Mead** in Main Street was broken into. The place was tossed and rummaged and the thiefs left with four pounds in coppers and some clothes.

Mr. William McTigue, shopkeeper of the same street, lost a pig which was killed and gutted at the back of his premises. During April numbers of dead bodies were carried past the offices of the *Telegraph*, borne on wattles. Poor women carried baskets of turf into the town on their backs because most of the asses had been slaughtered and eaten.

There were plenty of seed potatoes in the market during April because '47 had been free of blight. The potato crop had not been effected by the blight, but the yeild was too small to have any effect on the ongoing tragedy. Perhaps '48 might be a good year and the cycle of failure broken.

Many can no longer buy coffins. They lay their dead out on the streets and call for contributions from those passing by.

In May people were warned of Government spies moving among those who were doing public works. They were masquerading as overseers. They listened to every word spoken and reported back to Dublin. The Castle had its eyes everywhere.

In **Glenisland** and **Islandeady** the relieving officers were keeping food from those in need .

"The humble petition of the poor, starved and destitute widows, orphans and distressed persons of North Islandeady Electoral Division, who are in a state of starvation in consequence of being deprived of their relief meal on last week, and cut short of their allowance, while persons who are well off are getting full allowance."

Mr. Gallogly, the prisoner governor, had a problem on his hands. His jailhouse on the Westport Road was filled to capacity by vagrants who had deliberately smashed windows in the town and caused bother in order that they might be imprisoned and fed. The summer was coming and perhaps the dreaded fever might break out in the jail.

In May **Mr. John Mitchel**, proprietor of the *'United Irishman'*, was arrested and committed to Newgate to await his trial. It was rumoured that her Majesty the Queen would come to Ireland. **Frederick Cavendish** wondered if she would accept an invitation to Castlebar to see the condition of the town.

Meal cars brought food from **Westport** to **Castlebar** and from **Castlebar** to smaller towns and villages. The meal cars of **Mr. Charles O'Malley** were attacked at **Ross** by parties from **Turlough, Straide** and **Ross.** The people disappeared with bags of meal when **Constable Armstrong** of **Pontoon** police station and his men arrived. After a fatiguing mountain chase he succeeded in recovering a portion of the meal and he managed to take some prisoners.

In June rumour circulated in the town that **John**

Mitchel had been rescued by the French on his passage out to Bermuda. The weather was good and the potatoes in prime condition.

On Wednesday, June 21st a list of the eviction and clearances in the districts since the famine were published. Parish by parish the lists were given. In one parish 60 houses were levelled in May and people were thrown out on the road. The names and days and dates would have been forgotten had they not been recorded in the *Connaught Telegraph.*

In **Aughadrina** 289 were ejected. In **Balure** 53 ejected. In **Ballynabul** 53 ejected. In **Ardvanny** 68 ejected. In **Sarnaught** 59 ejected.

A leading article in *The Connaught Telegraph* begins with the headline "*Horrible, Horrible.*'

The reporter had visited the roads leading to the workhouse and records:

"*We saw hundreds of people crawling in from the countryside with asses, carrying in baskets starved children and crippled old men and women. They numbered at that time about 3,000 people. It is surprising that so many asses have survived.*"

The shops are now empty. The customers have been reduced to paupers by the landlords. The shopkeepers in turn are being reduced to the same state.

"*A gloom hangs over the town; it would seem a curse has been invoked on the inhabitants and that it has been responded to in the shape of locusts to devour the substance of the people. And this hunger outside the Poorhouse is only a drop in the ocean.*"

In early July houses were levelled on the estate of **Sir Roger Palmer**. They were pulled down by the 'Crowbar Brigade.'

Despite these scenes of horror and hardship the potato looked healthy.

The heat brings on the fever and a virulent type breaks out in **Castlebar** in Mid-July. On Friday night 8th June, **Christopher Walters** fell a victim in **Spencer Street**. A few hours before his death his appointment as relieving officer for **Ballin-tubber** had been confirmed.

On the 12th July a group of youths marched through the streets, headed by 3 persons, one carrying a tri-colour flag, composed of orange, green and while, streaming from a well shaped pike attached to a long handle. Another carried a board nailed to a pole inscribed "Castlebar Club.' The youth of **Castlebar** have adopted John Mitchel of Bermuda as their idol.

In August the potato blight strikes. The tops on the stalks became black and withered.

During the assizes week in August a young man said to be from America is brought into **Castlebar** from either **Ballindine** or **Claremorris** charged with giving orders for making pikes. He is placed in jail and refuses of give his name.

The total acreage of potatoes in 1848 was three times more than in 1847, but that summer was extremely wet. The blight raged again and the crops were lost.

"We have kept silent on this alarming subject as long as we could with propriety do so, not wishing to create alarm: but to continue so longer would be

unjust on our part, particularly when the disease, so far as the potato tops are concerned, is now universal- and what renders the case still worse, all the tops of the late plantings are becoming withered and black."

By August the potatoes are fast decaying. The grain is partially blighted and the drivers are out taking the cattle in payment of rents. The weather is wet. The rivers overflow and cover the low tillage fields. It is now too late to cut the turf.

And we read that the outdoor relief system has become snarled.

"The conditions of the poor of this town is at present ten times worse that it has been during any period of the past season. Our streets are crowded with crawling, wretched widows and orphans, deprived of relief. On Monday last the lamentations of these creatures was truly awful; they were they said, without relief for the last fortnight, although the guardians had left them on as deserving objects.

"Upon inquiry we learned that the issue of meal to the store, for their relief, was made during the last fortnight, but that instead of their being supplied, the meal still remains as an overplus, to the amount of close to fifteen cwt. weight. The issue of meal to the destitute did not commence until near dark on Saturday night, and the poor creatures were kept standing on the street, trembling, screaming and crying, up to eleven o'clock on that night, when many had to return home to their starving families, unsupplied.....We are told also that favourites draw meal three or four times a day, which they sell in the shops in this town, and this is done while the really destitute are sent empty away.

"We hear also of persons in our neighbourhood having acres of wheat, oats,barley and potatoes getting their relief meal in other person's names. They can well afford to have three chimneys to their dwelling, while their immediate neighbours lie down in hovels, without a bit of food to stay the gnawing hunger preying on their vitals."

Summer departs.

The hunger and lack of work enjenders intemperance and dissipation. Never did the town, we are told, exhibit such base depravity, through drunkenness; the back lanes are filled with poteen houses. The streets at all hours, both day and night were crowded with drunken wretches male and female of loose habits. The drunks make way to the graveyard and continue their drinking there.

On Thursday, August 14th, seven prostitutes were summoned before the magistrates in the Courthouse but were released.

"Never at any time within our memory has this town exhibited such base depravity, thro' drunkenness, as it does at present: Our back lanes are filled with potteen houses; our streets, at all hours, both day night are crowded with drunken wretches, male, and female, of loose habits.......To what a state are we reduced, when on Thursday last no less than seven prostitutes were summoned before the bench of magistrates."

In October the alarm spreads through the town that a boy had been beaten to death at the

Workhouse. It was not true. He had stolen milk and then resisted solitary confinement. For this he was beaten until he appeared dead. He was lucky. A boy had been beaten to death in the **Ballinrobe Workhouse**.

By mid-October the condition of **Castlebar** for starving beggars was horrible. The streets were rendered impassable by shoals of human skeletons, in a state of nudity. Some starving inhabitants took turnip rinds from the sewers and ate them.

"The conditions of Castlebar, from starving beggars, is truly horrible. The streets are constantly rendered almost impassable by shoals of human skeletons, in a state of nudity, importuning the inhabitants for food.

"To see these creatures of God's creation, picking up the filthy entrails of fish, turnip rinds etc., out of the filthy sewers and deavouring them with as much zest as if they had undergone the process of cooking, is indeed shocking."

Even the weather conspires against the poor and the starving.

"On Tuesday last and Wednesday we had a heavy fall of snow. Thursday and Friday frost; and on Saturday, Sunday , Monday, heavy rain, with a low and dark atmosphere. The winter is now fairly upon us."

But there is one just man to be found in all this despair and confusion. He is **Colonel M'Alpine** of **Windsor**. He had given his tenants work close to his residence.

"In all Ireland there is not a landlord who has

made more sacrifice to his tenantry as has this gallant and noble minded gentleman, nor one whose nobleness of conduct is more highly appreciate."

This landlord in never mention without praise.

In November the read the following of **Westport.** "In a former number we called attention to the very disgraceful practice now permitted with impunity in **Westport** , a town heretofore lauded by strangers for its beauty and cleanliness, but now ridiculed for its filth. We may be told it has not lost ground in regularity or cleanliness. We deny it; we ask is not Bridge Street an eternal disgrace to any towns in Ireland from the fact of its being daily and hourly rendered the theatre for slaughtering, scalding and scraping pigs? How often does it occur that these animals, in a dying state , run through the streets to the great danger of tumbling down all with whom the may come in contact?!

The December weather is bad. There are high winds, sleet and cold rain. On December 20th a terrible storm is reported. Slates are blown from the roofs. Lake Lannaugh water rushed through the gardens of the town and people took refuge in the upper storeys. This was the worst storm since January, 1839.

The year ended with this final note.

"The year 1848 found the countryside miserable indeed, and it is leaving you a thousand times worse."

And so 1848 ended. It was a dark year in every respect and there seemed no let up. The 'Crowbar brigade' would continue it's work turning villages into meadows using the stones of houses to build the bounding walls, emigration would continue. There would be hunger but not as much starvation. Forty-Nine would see among other things a gruesome hanging in the jail at Castlebar.

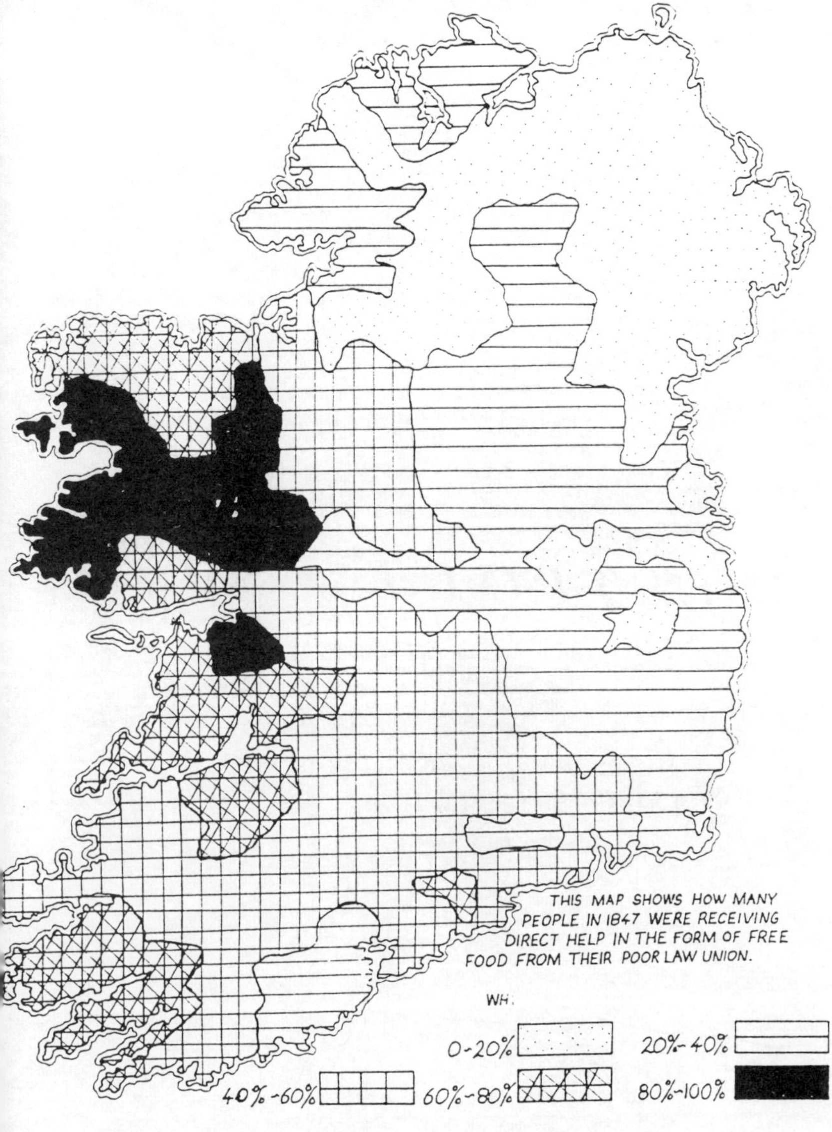

This map shows the number of people on relief in 1847.

WESTPORT DEMESNE
Wood Cot.
Holy Trinity Church
Westport Sch.
Lodge
266 A 1 R 14 P (including 1 21 water)
Waterfall
Westport Ho.
Church (in Ruins)
Grave Yard
Cahirnamart
Pollnacappul
Market Ho.
Octagon
Ball Alley
Church St.
Quay St.
Peter St.
James's Street
Shop St.
Bridge Street
High St.
Mill St.
John's Row
Quay Road
Reservoir
Dispy.
Union Workhouse
Hospital
Infantry Barrack
Toberavower
Workhouse Cemetery
Sea View
B.M. 25·8
B.M. 50·4
B.M. 54·8
B.M. 150·3
B.M. 121·9
B.M. 93·1

1849: Evictions and a Hanging.

The Famine has lasted for two years. Fever has taken its toll. The town is reeling from the experience. But despite all it continues to function.
The following is a comment on the appearance of Mayo at the beginning of 49.

"For a traveller from any part of Ireland going through Mayo the appearance of the county must present an awful picture; here and there the eye may rest on a few struggling cabins with smoke issuing from the doors, or through the rotten thatch; around those human habitation he can discover the ruins of innumerable cabins, monuments of English mislegislation, and Landlord oppression; and should he ask where are the people gone to who occupied these dwellings prior to the levelling process he might be told; some few have taken refuge in foreign lands; hundreds, while able bodied, must crawl about the ditches, the Poor Law affording no relief to such persons; thousands crowd into the towns in quest of food and shelter; and thousands more have hurried to untimely graves, in fields and bogs, without coffins, without shrouds."

All the powers of government and mismanagement and tyranny have been at work to destroy the marginalised. Things do not get better

The following notice has a ring of doom.

"On yesterday, according to notice served on the Relieving Officer by George Ormsby, chief Crowbar to Lord Lucan, the following individuals and their families, were hunted from house and home by his lordship's bailiffs. The townlands on which this cruel act was performed, are Upper and Lower Moneen, a short mile from Castlebar.

Lower Moneen — Pat Lavan, Owen Lavan, Bryan Lavan, Francis Blain, Winny Walsh, Bryan Carny, Pat Rily, John Rily (eldest daughter dead in the house) Jo Joyce, John Johnson, and Biddy Rily.

Upper Moneen — Jas Walsh, Margaret Killien, Widown (John) Comber, Biddy Mc Dermott, Patt Hopkins, Myles Walsh, Patt Walsh (Sen.), Mary Cleary, Mich. Colman, Patt Morrison, Peggy Dillon, Walter Mc Donell (eight in family lying in fever), Jas Maughan, Cath.O Hara, John Flynn, Mary Divir, Ann McHale, Patt Walsh and William Flynn.

The lists alone have a callous ring to them. Perhaps these people disappeared from the town. Perhaps they held tenaciously on and their descendants are here to day.

The people had endured the famine, the plague, injustice and neglect. Now they have to suffer eviction.

While evictions take place close to the town the town itself is subject to robberies. Doors and gates are taken from untenanted houses and windows are smashed so that people will get themselves admitted to jail. Better be fed within than starved without.

Mayo was now doomed to rival Skibberreen in famine and death. The hunger and the evictions continued. In January the Crowbar Brigade were out and about levelling the villages. The homeless had to make their way to the Workhouse or the ports. In January people were seen in Castlebar selling their furniture to obtain money for the passage to America and taking leave of their friends.

On Saturday, January 18, Mister Watson, rate collector for Castlebar and Islandeady, entered one of the houses in the town and seized an old churn containing a few quarts of buttermilk, some old clothes and an old torn gown for rates due. Joseph Grey, driver for Lord Lucan, and Roddy O Donal were attacked by men, women and children on Gallows Hill as they drove the cattle they had seized before them. Warrants were issued and the women were lodged in jail. The merchants at Westport raised the price of flour from 24 shillings to 30 shillings, giving as excuse that the yields were down in America. For three years they had taken advantage of the miserable condition of the people to fill their own pockets. In desperation carts carrying grain were plundered on their way from Westport.

This sad excerpt from a letter tells us how the poor suffer:

"On Sunday last, while walking up Gallowshill, in this town, my feelings were appealed to, on behalf of a poor family actually dying of starvation within a few acres of the Workhouse. Finding hunger was the cause of their ailment I supplied them with the price of food for that day and the next. The poor father declared to me they had not tasted of food since the previous Friday morning, save one half-

penny worth of raw turnips."

And the news from the Protestant Parson at Louisburg is also harrowing. In a long letter to the Connaught he sets out the distress of his flock. These few lines set the tone:

"One poor widow, a member of my flock, lost her husband and her husband's four children from the effects of starvation. Another poor widow, belonging to my congregation, lost her father, mother, and husband, by fever; and in the flames of fever she gave birth to a posthumous child........... there are graves in my churchyard have in my presence been assaulted by starving dogs."

On February 2Oth,twenty seven villages or townlands are named which had been levelled by the Crowbar Brigade. Levelling in most cases meant that the villages were wiped off the map. The stones from the houses were taken and used to build fencing walls for sheep runs.

And justice is seen to be done at Castlebar Jail by the governor, Mr. Gallogly. Though built to accommodate 188, it has in its cells some 584.

Murder .....5.
Manslaughter ..1
Burglary and Robbery..10
Uttering base coin 1
Sheep stealing 47
Larceny.... 90
For transportation .....42.
etc.

One prisoner will be hanged in public.

Deaths continued. We pick up the sad details of those who perished:

"We have just been informed that last week, a poor woman, with three children, turned out of the workhouse, on the out-door relief, which as stated to us, they never got, were found dead in a lime kiln on the townland of Collandeer, parish of Ballintubber, from fever and starvation, and in a decomposed state. The police got some straw thrown over them, and then covered the four with earth."

On March 7th, Mr. Stephen Donnelly, music master died. He was well regarded in the town and had conducted the Temperance Band. A military band marched before his funeral playing a polka piece arranged by the deceased. The piece chosen was regarded as being in very bad taste. In the same months a number of young men were discharged from the army. In Castle Street they tore the number of their regiments from the caps and cried out "Repeal of the Union."

The food supplied to the poor of the town at the time was little more than poison. Samples of the meal were brought to the offices for the "Connaught Telegraph" and once kneaded into dough they found that they could not endure the smell of it.

And now the vagrants, male and female, steal sheep and cattle and drive them in front of the police station, hoping to be caught and thrown in prison.

We read of the following death at Errew on march 14th:

"Some days since a poor man named Kelly, with his wife and two children, from the parish of Mayo, called at the Monastery of Errew for some charity, which was given them. Next day, at a little distance

from that excellent institution, the father and the children were found dead. The bodies were put into coffins provided by the Christian Brethren at Errew, who had them buried. The poor woman was also supplied by them with other little requisites befitting her weak condition. To those who enjoy even a little of the good things of this life we would say-take example from the Christian Brethren at Errew, who deny themselves for the comforting of God's afflicted."

The vice-guardians of the Union decided to open a cholera hospital in the town. The old coach stage at Ballymacragh is suggested as a better place. It is a mile and a half from the town and 2O beds could be laid down in the premises. In May the house of Mr. P. Walsh is converted into a "Calcutta" but as yet there is no evidence of cholera in town. Cholera would not appear but in order to keep the hospitals open and draw their pay any one suspected of the disease was taken in by the officials.

"On Thursday last one of the most cruel acts that could be was enacted in the town. Two children, a sister and a brother, creatures whose bed the night before were the flagstones, appeared, as a result of the cold, quite blue in the morning. The alarm went out that cholera had marked them. They were tumbled into a wheelbarrow and hurried to the cholera hospital. Later it was discovered that they suffered only from starvation.

And while all this was happening the Agamemnon, The William and Harry were waiting at Westport Quay for a prosperous breeze to take a thousand emigrants to America. On the 10th of May, the wind being favourable, the beautiful and well trimmed ships weighed anchor and were soon lost to view of many weeping persons along the shore and islands "whose friends had taken passage to a better land."

The levellers were in Rathbawn during the month. The houses were tumbled and the people thrown out on the road. They took refuge beneath the thatch and half-tumbled walls, but their rest was of short duration. The levellers returned and threw them out again and completely demolished the walls. And in villages further out the road conditions were worse. In one cabin was found three dead bodies, one lying dead for six days. another three days, another a day and a fourth person was found dying. And so it continued.

There was always fear of locating a cholera hospital in the center of Castlebar. The paper comes out against opening one in Main Street. Apparently a hotel is taken over for the purpose and riots follow.

"On the might of Sunday last, the young bloods of Castlebar laid siege to the Cholera Hospital in the Main Street, and with stones from the road, riddled ever pane of glass in front of the dreaded house. ......On Friday, Saturday, and Sunday, rumours prevailed that cholera had made its appearance in Stabball and Shruphane."

There was fear of Asiatic cholera all over the country. An infected man had arrived in Belfast from Edinburgh carrying the disease. He died in hospital but soon cases of cholera began to appear in the workhouse. The cholera was carried all over Ireland and reached its climax in May. Consequently one can understand the anxiety of people in Castlebar.

Apparently the town was not visited by the terrible disease.

"On the night of Thursday last the inhabitants of the town evinced their joy at the non-existence of cholera in Castlebar by lighting a large fire in the center of the Main Street, convenient of the house designed the "Cholera Hospital". Nothing could exceed the desire of the people to convince the rural population of the joyful fact that the town was never so free from sickness of any description and in one hour a towering heap of turf, bog, fir, tar barrel staves etc. was raised up in the street."

In July Count Strelitxke visited the town and is gratified by the work of the trade society to revive native manufacturers. He gave a large order for clothing, which for durability of wear and beauty of texture can scarcely be excelled by the machined cloth of Leeds and Manchester.

If Castlebar is free from the scourge of cholera not so Killala, Crossmolina, Ballina, Achill and Ballycroy;

"We have been told that cholera has appeared in those districts and that several poor persons have died. In those localities we fear many will become victims, as starvation had previously prepared the poor wretched population for this epidemic."

On the same page we learn that Mrs. Hession, assisted by Mrs. McNiff, intends giving a grand musical concert in this town on Monday night next, and on the following night at Westport. The musical and vocal powers of Mrs. McNiff and Miss Hession are already well known and appreciated.

A small light begins to glimmer in the darkness.

In August the Queen arrives at Cobh and is saluted by the thunder of guns from Spike Island. Next day she graciously condescend to christen the "Old Cove", Queenstown.

Now the potatoes are ready. When they reach the market the "infamous tribe of robbers and blood shedders" will not permit the farmers to sell them to anybody but themselves. Having bought the potatoes they sell them at double the price.

It is high summer now and the lords and ladies return to their estates in the west having wintered in London.

The crops are good and the potato seems to have survived the blight. Four sheep stealers try to escape from the jail. Ten convicts are transferred to Dublin and a man called Brogan is under sentence of death. The sentence is carried out on September 6th.

THE HANGING

"Here we must leave them for a short while and take a view of the 'finisher of the law' at his horrible work of preparation. He was a man in stature about five feet eight and by his own account 75 years old, but lively as a lamp-lighter in his movements. He wore the prison dress and a pair of light pumps. He also wore a mask over his face which he kept up except when he appeared before the immense crowd in front who he said 'were the most orderly audience he had ever appeared before'." In answer to a question he replied: "I have snigged off fifty persons in my life and this would make fifty one." Having all preparations nearly complete he said "he would do no more until he was sure of what he was going to get." Being satisfied on this point he remarked to the bystanders: "If he was promised twenty pounds and only got nineteen he would not feel pleased. If I bargained then everyman to his trade. This is mine. Let no reporter or sketcher for the press be admitted. I have no aversion for such gentlemen." Being told that there was none present he said: "I am now ready" and left the apartment with a shrug of his shoulders and a leer on his countenance, to enable the wretched culprit to advance without discomposure.

Upon a signal Brogan advanced, preceded by the Rev. gentlemen and followed by the religious brethren and a few gaol officers. His step was firm but instantly he entered the chamber and cast his eyes upon the apparatus of death his frame became agitated, his blood appeared to cease its circulation, his hands and face turned black, he closed his eyes and heaving a deep sigh he again knelt in prayer with the clergyman and with apparent zeal, invoked pardon for his sins and called upon God to have mercy on his soul. While kneeling the hangman entered and commenced his work by pinioning his arms. He uttered no sound during the ordeal save commending his soul to God which he did in Irish. He became so weak that he was obliged to be helped to a standing position, his eyes still closed. The white cap was placed on his head, when the clergymen quitted the apartment. The dreadful noose adjusted, the hangmen took him by the arms from behind and moved him before the trap. Here he seemed to stagger a little backward and the hangman in replacing him said: "Have courage man." In an instant the fatal bolt was drawn and the trap fell amid an awful shout from the bystanders, the great majority of whom were females and young boys.

"The body, having hung the usual time, was lowered onto a shelf and carried into the gaol where it was interred without going through the ordeal of surgical butchery.

"It is about 14 years since there was an exhibition of this nature in Mayo and it is the second execution since the present gaol was built."

The crowbar brigade moves to Stabball with Lord Lucan in attendance. Only the sooty gables are left standing. The potato disease progresses in several parts of the country and there is a complaint that the Tipperary teacher in the Workhouse is none too good at spelling. Men work under the town bridge by candlelight in order to finish their work and let the water run for the mill.

Colonel John Browne of Breaffy, who had been in Peninsular War and the Battle of Waterloo, dies.

In November there is a complaint about the condition of the streets. They were never so filthy in living memory, while down at the workhouse one hundred able bodied men are kept in idleness and spend the time looking at one another, gambling with cards and pitch and toss.

At the end of the year an optimistic note is sounded.

"Hearing no complaint against the potato disease for some time past, we take it for granted the virulence of the disease ceased with consumption of the early planting. Those at present brought to market one-tenth scarcely present indications of the complaint. "

There is hope for the future.

The year '49 ends. The pattern of emigration has been established, villages have been destroyed, small farmers have been thrown out on the side of the road, the Queen arrived in Ireland and there was a hanging in Castlebar jail.

The year '50 was a better one. It had to be!

CEMETERY
Union Workhouse
Hospital
Dispy
B.M.139·1
B.M.143·8
F.P.
206·2
200
132
F.B.
189·1
B.M.128·6
B.M.150·3
124
Pound
132
B.M.123·
148
B.M.142·4
B.M.128·1
ANTRIM STREET
LINEN HALL ST.
RICHARD STREET
B.M.150·9
F.P.
Constab
Presby
R.C.C.
R
B.M.122·8
P
127
1
18
Lake Lawn
Gas Works
NEW
F.P.
B.M.114·4
F.B.
B.M.110·4
CASTLEBAR
F.P.
Brewery
(in Ruins)
Meth. Ch.
THE GREEN
Church
Court House
Bank
B.M.146·8
B.M.140·
B.M.114·8
153
Old Church
Grave Yard
Stepping Stones
B.M.112·6
NEW
CEMETERY
B.M.120·7
INFIRMARY
MILITIA
BKS.
School
189
B.M.155·7
GAOL
Hospital
Weir
B.M.141·8
B.M.138·5

Common sort of Mayo Mud-Cabin.

1850: Light and Shade

In early January the landlords were following the judicial process by which people were driven from their holdings. One hundred ejectment orders were placed in front of the judges by the Marquis of Sligo, Lord Kilmain, the Earl of Lucan, Sir William O'Malley, John Knox and Cononel Charles Knox.

Such was the depopulation of the countryside that the town was overflowing with paupers who had no work and no food. This is the scene in front of the Workhouse on January 15.

"That day was awfully cold, a piercing north wind and frost on the ground. Before the Workhouse at least 600 to 800 applicants for relief, young and old, some in baskets in the last stage of disease brought on by starvation and cold. They sat for hours on the uncomfortable and frost-hardened yard, before the boardroom waiting for the hour of scrutiny, whether they were to get food and live for some time longer or be denied and crawl off to die by the wayside."

At two o'clock the guardians descended from the boardroom to the hall, when the names of the suiters for food began to be called. We were forcibly struck by a remark made by the gallant and humane Colonel McAlpine. On looking at the awful spectacle before him, he exclaimed."I thank God there are no tenants of mine here.....Out of the several hundred that day seeking food and shelter, about sixty human beings of all ages were blessed with being taken into the house or placed on the out-door relief."

During the terrible years Colonel M'Alpine had treated his tenants with regard and favour. Only a wing of his great house exists today in Windsor. When he left for London in January, Cavendish had this to say of him.

"In Mayo there is not a family whose departure will be more felt by the poor than that of the gallant Col. M'Alpine. As a landlord, in acts of liberality to his tenantry he has but few equals this side of Saint George's Channel; while from his extensive estates in Mayo there is not a pauper in any of our workhouses."

The Lanack froze over and the notables of the town were seen skating across the iced surface. While the notables skated "their lady loves, with fluttering hearts, sparkling eyes, and ruby pouting lips encouraged the gay aspirants."

Even the mitchers from the schools enjoyed themselves during the frozen spell.

The Castlebar Industrial Society, now well established at Newtown, held a dinner in February.

By now it employed 300 people. Clad in tweed spun by themselves they sat down to a dinner at Flynn's Hotel. "Immediately over the chair was suspended a beautiful painting of "A daughter of Erin her hand mechanically on the chords of an

Irish harp; at her right hand appeared the Irish wolfhound apparently elated with the harmony of the music drawn from the instrument of his mistress. On top of this unique piece of native art was inscribed ENCOURAGE IRISH MANUFACTURE; ERIN MY COUNTRY; GOD SAVE THE QUEEN, LOVE, PEACE AND PLENTY."

In the county there were now over six thousand on relief. There were thousands of others who had been unable to receive relief so hunger and starvation continued. But the paper no longer dwells upon these things. In a sense the county is emerging slowly from the terrible days of the famine. The courts proceedings and the trials are well covered. The range from the sublime to the ridiculous.

In March Shambles Lane ran red with pig blood as the victuallers had no slaughter house to kill their animals.Lorenzo Marra was brought to Castlebar from Galway to act as interpreter for Giovanni Molchotich whose ship had been pirated off the coast of Inis Boffin. Snow fell several feet thick, and there was ice skating on Lanach and Black Lough.

In April the crowbar brigade was active again. "The proceedings of the Crowbar Brigade within the last week shall be remembered in this neighbourhood for ages to come. Who of our Mayo readers had not some time or other admired the beautiful dwellings in Upper, Middle and Lower Annagh on the banks of Lanack, near Clonkeen, about three miles from Castlebar. There is not one stone upon another in any of these three villages.

All, have been raised with the earth by process of law and the aid of the Crowbars."

"On Easter Saturday morning, a cold and rainy day, the Crowbar Brigade moved through Linenhall Street, fully armed, and made their way to Rathbawn. Soon the houses were tumbling down. One young boy pleaded with the levellers.

"My poor mother is dying in the bed. I know not what to do with her. I wanted to leave her in bed until the priest anoints her. There are seven of us since yesterday morning, without breaking our fast. ......After hearing the poor boy's pitiful recital of his grievance we advanced with him to his mother's bedside, which was in the kitchen, around the fire place of which were half-crouched five children crying with fear and hunger. Half seated in the bed, in the act of being removed therefrom by her daughter, was the dying mother who exclaimed, "Oh, Sir, they will not leave me in the house until I'm anointed; will you ask them to leave me in the house until I die, which is not far off. The sight was too trying to look on long , and we hurried out to the superintendent of the leveller, who we addressed on behalf of the sick skeleton we had just left, requesting for the love of God, he would not tumble the house until the priest had performed his office with her."

On Friday, April 12, Connaught Rangers moved into town to the sound of cheek music. They were cheered as they passed through the streets. The Rev. Stoney is accused in Mayo of proselyting. Apparently every inducement in soup, bread and clothes was held out to the children of poor Roman

Catholics to inveigle them to change from the religion of their parents.

"They are taught to look upon the faith and discipline of the Catholic Church as damnable and idolatrous. The holy days and the fast days of their church are held forth to them as mummery and the invention of crafty priests."

The deepening of the river caused considerable bother in the town. Young children played without much care for life on the temporary bridge at the back of The Grove. The flow of the river had been stopped and now it had been turned into a receptacle for unmentionable night soil of no less than four Auxiliaries (Workhouses). Archdeacon McHale had a narrow escape when his gig hit sewer flaggings and he was thrown onto the road.

In May the weather worsened. For several nights the ground was hardened by frost. There is sleet in the town and snow on the mountains.

Nevertheless the markets in Westport are well supplied with potatoes, and the prices are moderate.

Now the Crowbar Brigade turns to the islands.

"The island of Innishturk, in the western seas of the far-famed tenant-exterminating Mayo and the property of the tenant loving Earl of Lucan has been the scene of much lamentation and weeping within the last eight or nine days during a visit to the island by a section of his Lordships' Crowbar Brigade, accompanied by the Deputy Sheriff and a posse of the constabulary... Our informant states that out of four cartrons on which stood eight villages, only a few houses were left standing for the accommodation of care-takers, and that between four and five hundred humans beings were thus deprived of home and shelter, and left exposed to the cold sea breezes on an island surrounded by the Atlantic and nine miles from the nearest point of the main land.

It was learned in June that the brig Jane bound for Westport with a general cargo consigned for the merchants of that town was boarded by several boat crews from the main land, off Eagle Point, and plundered of an immense quantity of flour.

There was music on The Mall in June provided by the military band and this was to continue during the whole summer. There were very large amounts of potatoes on sale at the market and poteen whiskey fetched 12 shilling a quart. Trout and salmon were also on sale. People were advised to eat them with poteen sauce. In the same month The Ohio Minstrels arrived in the town.

But there was little singing outside the workhouse in Ballinrobe. Starvation is whittling away the weak.

"On Thursday last the Ballinrobe Guardians were besieged by vast crowds of starving creatures, looking for relief. It was melancholy to behold the number of skeletons and their frightful appearance. The guardians were obliged to give a good many of them out-door relief, having no workhouse accommodation. .....There are , we understand, at present in the workhouse about 30 deaths a week; and many prefer dying by the roadside to entering the house, as was the case of a poor woman who died on the public street of that town on Thursday last....."

Mr. Robert Dillon Browne M.P. died and the "Connaught" takes up the cause of Ousley Higgins, a candidate for the vacant seat in Parlimaent. Landlords rush to have their names registered for the coming elections but they are told "the law is quite explicit, gentlemen. You must be registered six months before you can vote for a member of parliament. The law makes no difference in that respect, between a fifty pound and a ten pound freeholder."

Ousley Higgins is elected. He was put in by the small freeholders. Their names are known and the landlords seek vengeance.

"A considerable fund had been already raised in England and in this country to protect and ameliorate the sufferings of the families of those who may be prosecuted for having supported Mr. Ouseley Higgins at the elections. We have had several communications, detailing acts committed by certain heartless and cruel landlords against freeholders for voting against their orders."

In September Rev. Stoney takes a blast from the "Connaught."

"For some Sundays in succession this Rev. Gentleman amuses his congregation by his wholesale abuse of the Roman Catholic Religion. He should have some consideration for the feelings of some of his congregation, the children of Roman Catholics, who for worldly advancement, joined his flock."

September and the town is described as a national disgrace. The flags covering the sewer flowing from the infirmary close to Carr's well in Castle Street needed repairing.

The archway and the sewers of the town had not been equalled anywhere for filth, and the passage leading from the town to the chapel by Shambles Street was an abomination.

The Brass Castle, where once lived Polly Corcoran and Mocky Pindle, like many of the old buildings in the town, was in a ruinous condition.

In September there was wholesale smuggling of illicit whiskey into the town, carried to purchasers by milk women and egglers.

"We would also warn persons having a fancy for the mountain dew as ten to one some of those, nay all of them, may be "Molly O'Briens' informers in the pay of the revenue."

At Carr's Well the only well in the town, which was undergoing repairs at the time, a reporter found a fisher woman holding a basket of rotten herrings over the spring while a little boy stood in the well pouring water over the basket which worked it's way through into the spring again.

The wind came cold on Sunday, October 6, carrying with it a freezing rain.

Despite the harsh biting weather the pauper children were marched from one of the Auxiliaries to the parish church, thinly clad and chattering with cold.

The cold and stormy weather continued battering the corn crops. The farmers had waited, as was the custom, for the corn to shed before reaping and they were caught.

The digging of the potato commenced. The crop

had partially failed.

'In many instances more than one half of the potatoes, called lumpers, are rendered useless even for pigs. Protestants, another strain of potato, have escaped the disease'.

At the end of the month it was reported that a rich coalmine had been discovered in the estates of Lord Kilmaine, in the neighbourhood of the town and an extensive mine was also reported on the estate of Thomas Phillips on Cloonmore.

These reports suggested to the editor that a railroad should be built from Galway to Castlebar.

When the news runs out the editor returns to one of his favourite subjects: the conditions of the streets of the town. Perhaps the description is exaggerated but the streets are far from inviting.

"In all Ireland we believe there cannot be found a more filthy town that we live in. Turn where you may, nothing meets the eye but heaps of nuisance. In the ruins of the old meat shambles, leading to the Chapel, may be seen mountains of abomination, the odour of which is sufficient to draw down a plague on the inhabitants. To add to this evil, the wall has been nearly all removed, by means of which the eye is instantly attracted to this depot of manure. The streets of the town present no better appearance- a foot passenger can hardly make his way through the mud and mire-add to this the incessant flow of obnoxious water and rotten dung from archways into the streets, and you have a picture of Castlebar".

But despite the conditions in the streets of Castlebar the Swinford Races will go ahead.

Ousley Higgins has presented the organizers with a cup worth Fifty Sovereigns.

In November the paper had the pleasure of announcing James Foy, citizen of the town, had been appointed to the important office of Consul for the United States.

The state of the workhouse is written up in December.

In main house......487
'Infirmary.........219
No. 1 Auxiliary ....167.
Sleeping in No.2 Auxiliary 290
In shed no 1 .... 224.

A school inspector has visited the union and furnished the Guardians with this report.

"The male teacher is very well qualified, as regards both his literary acquirements and his method of conducting his business.

The female teacher is tolerably well qualified.

The male school, which I examined very carefully, has improved very much since my last visit. The answering of the pupils on all the subjects was highly satisfactory, and the discipline and general arrangements of the school excellent."

Final arrangements had been made in Ballina that one of the splendid new steamers would ply between that town and the ports of England. The era of the sailing ships was drawing to it's close.

The year ended with hail, rain, sleet and snow. The mountains were covered with snow and the streets were impassible from mire and sludge. Things are beginning to improve despite the bad weather.

THE POOR LAW UNIONS OF COUNTY MAYO

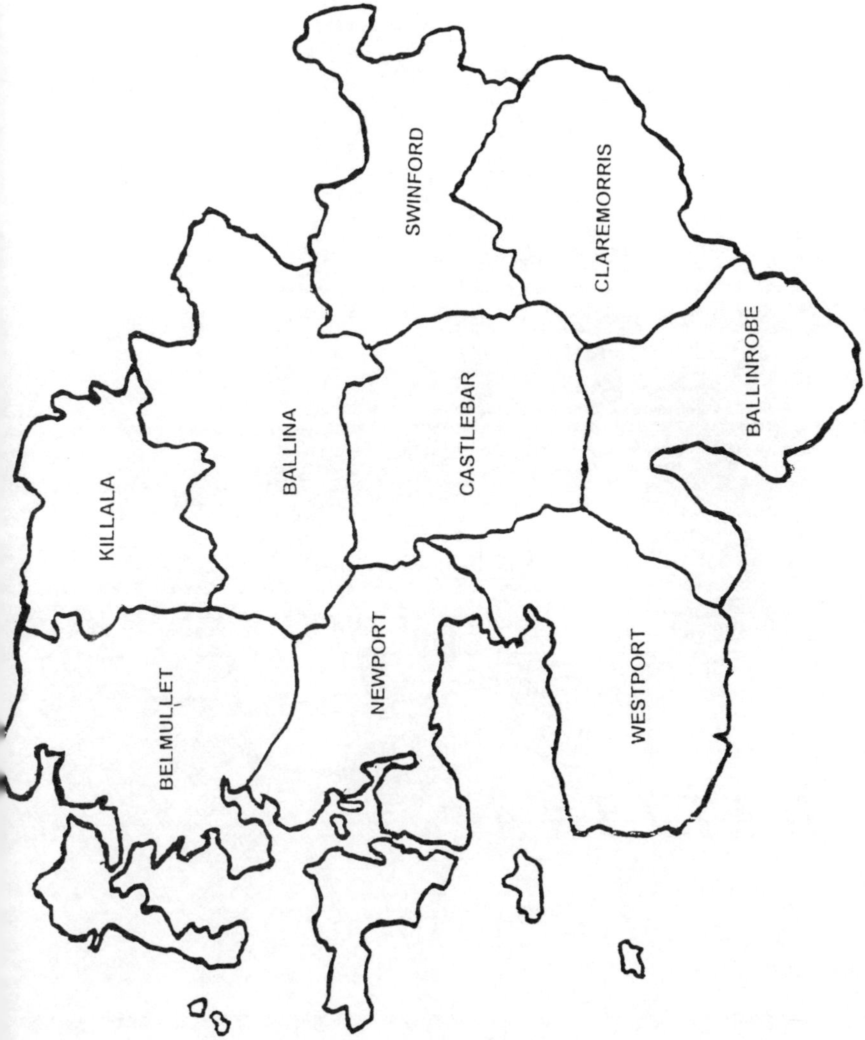

St. Patrick's Rock
St. Patrick's Well
Fert Echtra (Site of)
Princess' Grave
B.M. 66·8
Sluices
S.P
Smithy
100
46
F.B.
M.P 167
50
Brick Field
Burial Ground
Circular Road
All Hallows Convent
Crossmolina (Old) Road
School
Fever Ho
Quarry
Garden Street
Fair Gr.
Union Workhouse
A
546
B.M. 72·6
Dispy
Workhouse Road
F.B.
58
Arthur Street
School
Bury Street
Bridewell
Court Ho.
B.M. 57·8
BALLINA
S.P
50
Mally Villa
49
Cricket Ground
Cork Mill
Palmyra Cott.
Carrowcushlaun West
Primrose Hill
Saw Mill
Gas Works
Weir
F.B.
B.M. 43·1

1852: RUMOURS OF GOLD HIT CASTLEBAR

The year begins with an attempt to revive the linen trade which has gone into the decline. It is discovered that there are only eighty looms in Castlebar out of the hundreds which were formerly in use. Mr. Pinkerton of Westport attended a meeting in Castlebar Linen Hall, where he employed a great number of linen weavers, to whom he supplied yarn. He also furnished such weavers as stood in need of loom gear, the price of which he was satisfied to take from them at 6d a week.

In January there is fear of a war with France.

A widow names Harriet McKinley was murdered near the gaol. A pair of regimental mittens found beside her are traced to the 41 depot in the Castle Barracks. A soldier Pat Cuff is taken into custody and placed in the military lock-up to await trial.

February 11 carries the following report from Westport.

"We thought when we read of the brutal, ignorant and lust-loving potmen of London burning the image of the Mother of God in their streets that they became a match for the chief of the fiends of hell. But what shall we say of a man (claiming to be a clergyman) who the other day in

Westport exhibited at a gathering of people, what he called a wafer, similar to that used in the Host of the Catholic Church. This wafer he held up to his audience and to show that it possessed neither life not blood he dissected it with his knife and next with holy zeal he rubbed it beneath his clerical boot in the dirty earth.

"Shame, eternal shame upon you, Catholics of Westport."

March the 3rd we discover that Thomas Moore died at Sloperton Cottage at 72 years of age. He gave Ireland its greatest songs during the nineteenth century. In 1798 he narrowly escaped being involved with Emmet and others in a charge of sedition. His Irish melodies were immensely popular and proved to be the most lasting of his works. It was these works which brought attention to those who circulated in the drawing rooms of London that there was an old culture in Ireland steeped in a Celtic past. They are still sung and still carry the emotional idealism of the nineteenth century and a romantic patriotism which haunts the mind.

Recruitment is stepped up because of the threatened war with France..

"Since the arrival of the buffs in this town a degree of liveliness pervades the streets owing to their occasional beating up of recruits, a tolerable number of which have already joined; even in the workhouse the melodious notes of fife and drum have evoked a spirit of gallant ambition, and some young lads have joined from thence, while many more regret their youth and height which prevents them from being enlisted."

There is an air of confidence among farmers and the fact that '51 brought only partial failure to the crop gives the feeling that next harvest will bring less failure. This means that the Workhouse can be economically supplied by local produce thus keeping the money of the rate payers in the area.

"And the area does need money flushed into it. Several shops are shuttered in Castlebar. In Market Street alone fourteen houses are closed and the children play ball against the shutters."

George Henry Moore of Moore Hall has been active in the House of Commons. His attitudes and politics can be gathered from the following speech.

'What has the landlord-made law done? It has covered the face of this fine and fertile country with the levelled roofs and blackened walls of thousands and the tens of thousands of the cabins and cottages and farm houses on which the infamous Crowbar Brigade has executed its merciless commands. Where are they now? It has hunted neighbours, relatives, brethren, sisters, beloved children away from the land of their birth and of their affections.' Moore was a gentleman of great courage and one of the great orators of the House of Commons. His political life was both hectic and tragic; his death at Moore Hall melancholic.

During the last years and after the famine the landlords were active in sweeping the tenants off the land. Many found their way into exile and many carried the memory of starvation and eviction with them. These images were to lodge deep in the Irish-American consciousness.

Now that the spring is here there is a scarcity of hands to do the work. Several boys had to be taken from the Workhouse to help with the labour.

'But the old hands in the poorhouse it seems, have taken out a lease for life and will not be persuaded even by the prospect of wages, to quit the house. The number of those worthless drones are but few, and we trust means will be adopted to make out work for them.'

The weather comes good in April and there are high hopes held out that there will be an influx of tourists.

'The inducements held out to the English tourists, by means of return tickets, are so strong this summer that we have no doubt Ireland will enjoy a large sprinkling of English visitors, who it is needless to say, shall be welcome with an Irish 'Céad Míle Fáilte.'

The weather was indeed too dry in April and the drainage works contributed to the fact that every spring in the town and suburbs dried up. It is now time for emigration and a great number of respectable farmers with their families and luggage pass through the town on their way to Westport.

Matthew Gallagher writes from Australia.

'The colony has undergone a sudden change. Gold is found in abundance. Good wages are given and meat is very cheap. It is a splendid country with plenty of work for all kinds of labour and good pay. I am getting 31.1Od per annum as coachman.'

A partial fall of rain relieves the draught and news arrives that orders have been issued for the release of the Irish State prisoners, Smith, O'Brien, John Mitchell and their companions subject to the conditions that they are not to set foot in the United Kingdom again.

There may be gold in Australia but there are dreams of gold in Mayo.

'We have witnessed the successful test made a few days since by our talented townsman, John Atkinson, on a piece of granite over three-fourths of which that gentleman has reduced to copper and tin. The area occupied by the strata, from which the specimens tested have been taken, covers miles of Mayo. You have each of you, gentlemen, California on your estates.'

The report does not go unnoticed. An owner of very valuable mining properties in Cornwall offers to invest money if the Mayo find proves viable.

The evictions continue. Villages are destroyed on the property belonging to Sir Roger Palmer. "The Crowbar Brigade move in headed by a gaunt figure, somewhat resembling the orangutan which made the tour of the county some years ago and will be remembered by the name 'Happy Jerry.'"

There was discovered in the bed of the lake near Rehins, a number of low decanters whose exteriors were coated with tin and copper along with a number of ancient canoes, 17 feet long and four across, hollowed out of huge blocks of black oak wood. Hunters for hidden treasure made their way to Boyd's Island, but beyond finding one silver spoon and two pieces of silver coin nothing was discovered but numerous beds of bone. They have been taken away to be manufactured into bone dust. Perhaps they had come across a Bronze Age site. If so, there must be still remnants of this settlement in the area.

Mr. Atkinson continues his discoveries of ore.

'We have permission to state that four miles around the town on the estate of Lord Lucan a rich field of copper, tin and other minerals, which from the surface appearance and the result of his chemical operations, he believes, to be sufficiently prolific to enrich all Ireland."

In June election fever mounts.

'Our battle cry shall be Ireland and Tenant Rights. Down with the Crowbar Brigade and their chiefs. Hurrah for Moore and Higgins,' the slogans proclaim. Even in these slogans we can see the beginnings of a land league and the emergence of a new political grouping.

The election fever mounts and in mid-July a troupe of the 11th Huassars, commanded by Major Douglas and Lieutenant Inglis, arrive in town to be stationed here during the elections.

Patt Cuff is placed in the dock, tried for murder and condemned to death. The judge, having donned his black cap, pronounced sentence...

"That you Patrick Cuff be taken from the place where you now stand to the place from whence you came, the gaol , thence with your irons taken off, to the common place of execution, the gallows and hanged by the head, and your body buried within the precincts of the gaol and that sentence be executed upon you on the 1st September next and may the Lord have mercy on your soul.'

The news of the sentence is soon forgotten when

news gets around that the freeholders who are to vote in the elections are kidnapped. The landlords are going to make sure that their men are elected.

'An unconstitutional assault on many of the electors has been made. Many of the electors have been carried off by the Darbyites of Mayo and placed in confinement in the local Bastilles in Castlebar, Foxford and Westport in order to make them vote for Colonel McAlpine the avowed supporter of the enemies of the Catholic Religion.

No. 1 Bastille is at Michael Clarke's House in Spencer St. where, contrary to the law, they have been supplied with a side of beef and other refreshments.

But despite the pressures Moore and Higgins are returned as members of Parliament for Mayo.

The political times are changing. Moore will later help found an Independent Party, which will be destroyed by parliamentary bribes. Later Parnell will use a similar party which, successful for a time, is destroyed by the Parnell-Kitty O Shea scandal.

In the Castlebar gaol Patrick Cuff prepares for hanging but the sentence of death is never carried out. It is commuted and he is sentenced to transportation for life.

By August the break-water at the new bridge near the Grove is almost completed. But as the farmers watch their fields they are haunted by the memories of the recent years.

'The probability of another failure in the potato crop continues to alarm the people and the exodus from this part of Ireland is going on at a rapid rate.

Farmers are disposing of their effects. Labourers are likewise flying with their families to England and Scotland."

Emigration is now a familiar thing.

In August Mr. Atkinson has this to say of his discoveries. 'I have made an immense sacrifice of time and property in making my discoveries and I will not impart my knowledge, to enrich others. without receiving the compensation I am fully entitled to. I know where they abound, but without my reward they shall rest undisturbed.'

In September one of the soldiers, lately returned from California said he observed gold in the gravel being quarried at the Grove Bridge. Gold fever hit the town. It was too late to do anything. Whatever gold lay in the river-bed was now covered with stones and mortar.

'Did you hear that a year ago the sappers and miners told the Government that there were shoals of gold in the river and that to protect it Lord Derby is getting the place closed up' somebody said.

'That shows us the English will never let us rise' someone else commented.

In the same month the Duke of Wellington, the man who defeated Napoleon, died and an era was brought to a close.

In November buyers were purchasing potatoes in Castlebar for the Dublin markets and driving up the prices. It was a time of improvement for the shopkeepers.

Of the fair someone remarked. 'A most excellent one. We had not sufficient hands to attend the customers. There can be no second opinion on the matter. The times are visibly improving. We must receive the pounds from those you could not squeeze the shillings or pence from in years gone by.'

The editor rejoices at the arrival of the good times but writes. 'We the newspaper proprietors would desire to experience a portion of the improvement from those who have outstanding debts. We desire not if possible to increase the fees of lawyers in seeking what is our own.'

In December the Marchioness of Sligo dies of lingering consumption. Born at Constantinople in 1842, she lived only for 28 years and left one daughter.

It was good year for some a bad year for others. The villages were levelled, the countryside depopulated and patterns of emigration set down. There was the suggestion that Castlebar was surrounded by untold mineral wealth and Patrick Cuff, condemned to death, was reprieved and sentenced to transportation for life.

PARISH	POPULATION 1841	POPULATION 1851	HOUSES 1841	HOUSES 1851
Achill	6392	4950	1387	956
Addergoole	7379	5085	1313	949
Aghagower	12235	6511	2298	1302
Aghamore	7675	6097	1427	1241
Aglish	10464	9135	1835	1196
Annagh	7904	6105	1477	1194
Ardagh	2621	1497	463	263
Attymass	3435	2431	651	463
Balla	1934	1272	331	224
Ballinchalla	1722	1420	311	275
Ballinrobe	10115	9326	1884	1303
Ballintober	7199	3438	2217	672
Ballyheane	4032	1987	798	405
Ballynahaglish	5397	3393	956	664
Ballyovey	4505	3073	792	590
Ballysakeery	6034	2951	1068	571
Bekan	5589	4724	1053	886
Bohola	4301	2907	737	561
Breaghwy	2452	1136	456	218
Burriscarra	1681	913	296	162
Burrishoole	11942	7528	2217	1254
Castlemore	2944	2831	520	508
Cong	5359	3839	999	758

Crossboyne	6702	4963	1195	953
Crossmolina	12221	7236	2219	1278
Doonfeeny	4819	2720	865	491
Drum	4127	2732	758	548
Inishbofin	1612	1047	288	196
Islandeady	8463	4699	1556	921
Kilbeagh	9963	9733	1784	1774
Kilbelfad	3681	2296	629	423
Kilbride	1963	1144	329	193
Kilcolman (Claremorris)	9451	7421	1670	1323
Kilcolman (Costello(Part)	4365	4151	754	717
Kilcommon	7456	5255	1285	952
Kilcommon (Erris)	17000	12253	2935	2079
Kilconduff	7072	6909	1287	1140
Kilcummin	2791	1552	500	293
Kildacommoge	3923	2234	710	420
Kilfian	6040	3348	1094	589
Kilgarvan	4158	3194	785	580
Kilgeever	12573	6892	2309	1263
Killala	3253	2919	593	400
Killasser	6962	4852	1240	949
Killedan	6410	5158	1168	1047
Kilmaclasser	3548	1614	630	315
Kilmainebeg	1491	895	255	174

Kilmainemore	4877	3293	898	645
Kilmeena	7876	5108	1398	929
Kilmolara	1296	864	243	180
Kilmore (Erris)	9428	7379	1720	1106
Kilmoremoy	7028	6393	1318	1163
Kilmovee	5844	5882	1095	1120
Kilturra (Part)	1350	1023	259	200
Kilvine	2236	1697	392	308
Knock	3374	3174	616	600
Lackan	2943	1176	511	207
Manulla	2336	1387	404	241
Mayo	4179	2379	751	734
Meelick	3915	2692	680	521
Moorgagagh	627	294	112	54
Moygownagh	2107	1181	369	177
Oughaval	13441	13282	2385	1741
Rathreagh	1664	790	287	146
Robeen	3544	2522	648	505
Rosslee	1283	694	216	143
Shrule	5087	3004	876	565
Tagheen	3084	2051	582	389
Templemore	4251	2387	770	434
Templemurry	1291	514	242	83
Toomore	3744	2498	707	500

1851: LORD LUCAN PICKS PAUPERS FOR EXPORT

The year opened with some local excitement.

"On the night of Sunday last, while evening service was being performed in the Protestant and Methodist Church a man, apparently insane from drink, ran through the streets pursued by his daughters and others calling out "stop him, he is going to drown himself in the lake.'

"I am going to drown myself in the beautiful Lanack", he called as people collected about him. Reaching the graveyard he hesitated.

"Go on you are a coward. Rob not the devil of his due," the crowd told him.

"I am now at the grave of my first wife and will stop to take my leave of her" he told them.

"Say a prayer for her", they called. "It's time for you."

He stood and recited some of Cato's speeches before his living audience and beside the grave of his wife. The police arrived and put him in the blackhole for the night.

During the same month the police were trying to discover who carried off the brass knockers from several respectable houses in the town.

In late January, Cloggernagh, a village as beautiful as that described in 'The Deserted

Village', is reduced to rubble.

"Cloggernagh stood in a beautiful valley, nearly midway between Castlebar and Westport on the brow of the picturesque Lanack, near Islandeady. Perhaps in all Mayo there was not a prettier summer scenery for the eye to feast on that was here presented.

"On the eminence above the village, stood a national school, about ten years erected, wherein the youth of the village were being educated. Through the village, or rather where the village stood, runs a stream on the bosom of which has worked for years a manor mill for the accommodation of the villagers.

"By what infatuation has the landlord been beset thus to lay in ruins this beautiful village, and drive to the highways or into the workhouse those villagers with their families at this inclement season."

And at the workhouse the Earl of Lucan had the healthy female paupers from the age of 15 to 18 collected in the poorhouse yard for the purpose of selecting from them a number to be sent out to the thriving colony of Australia.

In February the Castlebar Industrial Society held it's third anniversary dinner. A brass band was in attendance and the toasts are interesting.

"The Queen and may God bless her."

The band plays God save the queen.

"Gentlemen the next toast is to the health of one of the greatest men the world has produced since the days of St. Peter, Pius 1X"

The band plays 'Rule Britannia'.

"To the memory of Daniel O'Connell.'

Band plays 'Remember the glories of Brian the Brave'."

"To the most Rev. Dr. McHale, liberal benefactor of our society."

Band plays 'See The Conquering Hero Come'.

In March people are warned against going near the ruins of Mugan's old house, which, if not well guarded, will unquestionably be the cause of somebody's death.

And week after week the Workhouse is beset by unfortunate contractors and poor tradesmen, in quest of money long overdue. They have little chance of receiving their money as the Workhouse is broke.

Emigration continues from the Workhouse. It is different now. Those who have fled the country have sent back passage money for the children. For some of them the dark days are over.

'While one generation is being buried in the Workhouse cemeteries, the rising one is making preparation for joining friends in another more prosperous place where the clang of the crowbar is only heard clearing for new buildings, not in levelling the inhabitations of men."

Now that the great fair has opened in London it is suggested that a Mayo invention should be on display.

"It is a machine for carrying the exterminated tenantry of the head sexton of the horrible Charnel House to the burial grounds.

It is built in the shape of a coffin with a sliding bottom. The dead man can be pitched into it without distinction of age or sex. It is conveyed, when well-packed, and placed over a spacious grave where the bottom can be withdrawn and the ill-fated corpse let fall into the cavity. When this melancholy operation is performed the machine is conveyed back to the Charnel House where the doctor can provide another cargo."

A policeman called Murphy finds himself in jail for bigamy. He married a woman from Pontoon although formerly married to a lady from Erris.

In June the drainage works were in progress at Rahins. No Castlebar man need apply. When they arrived, looking for work,they were reminded of the side they took in the recent local elections. "You had your day," Mr. Browne told them. "Now I'm having mine."

In the same month the Avon sailed for Inishturk, where the sheriff's officer's ejected nearly the whole of the inhabitants from their houses and demolished them.

In July at the Quarter Sessions 500 ejectment orders were processed by the men of the law. This meant that The Landlords were legally entitled to throw 2,300 human beings onto the road. Here is what happened to one such person.

"On Saturday last the executioners of the law in Lord Lucan's service tumbled into the street the little household effects of the widow Cauley of Struphane, a poor creature about 80 years of age, and put double padlocks on the door of her cabin. They acted in the same cruel manner towards her daughter and family residing in the adjoining houses. On Saturday and Sunday nights this old woman, with her two daughters and grandchildren, had to sleep out in the street. Those thus cruelly treated by a High Church Protestant are members of the same persuasion as himself."

The railroad has opened up Connaught. For Galway and the outlying areas it brings new revenue. The opening of the Galway Railroad brings a large influx of tourists.

"Numerous gentlemen of note from England and Scotland and distant parts of Ireland have visited Connemara, to enjoy the sea air and romantic mountain scenery of that wild but beautiful country."

A letter is received from Australia. The paupers from the Workhouse have finally reached their destination. The letter we are told is of a most cheering nature.

While preparing the 23th of August, 1851, edition of the paper, the editor observe from the window two young men on a cart on their way to the infirmary, apparently in a dangerous state from the sudden explosion of a rock into which powder had been put at the drainage in Islandeady.

Comes the beginning of September and the extension to Colonel James McAlpine's residence in Windsor is finished.

All who worked on the extension, mechanics, masons, carpenters, painters, plasterers, smiths, nailers and labourers are invited to dinner. It is a very happy occasion and a relief from the dark and dreary times.

"The dinner comprised, roast and boiled beef, mutton, fowl etc. and every luxury of the season with a plentiful supply of porter and other liquor. Refreshments consisted of tea, coffee, confectionery, fruit, bread and food of every description. They danced until four in the morning. Poor Ireland, wretched Connaught, had we many such men as Colonel McAlpine living amongst us."

Mention is made in September of mineral deposits close to Castlebar.

"Now my Lord has it ever occurred to you, that on the estates of the Earl of Lucan in the neighbourhood of Castlebar may be found mines of copper, lead, tin and iron with many other valuable properties including manganese, and the best description of earth in Europe for the manufacture of delph and crockery ware."

Emigration continues. It is suggested that in a few short years if the flow continues Mayo will be one vast desert, her hills, her valleys and majestic rivers the themes for the rhapsodies of the exiled Irish in happier lands.

December ends with a visit to the Workhouse.

"On Thursday last we visited the cooking apartment of this establishment, where we examined the food being cooked for the pauper inmates; the stirabout was good and substantial and the gruel was found to be extremely good and nutritious.

"In the clothes-stores we also observed, in good presentation, a large supply of clothing, including friezes, flannels, blankets, sheeting, tweed, linen, all (except the blankets) manufactured by the paupers in the house. There were 300 children in the female school and great credit is due to Miss

Wilson."

The times were still bad but they had improved a little.

A typical cabin at the time of the famine.

1853.....Let there Be Light.

This year marks the arrival of gas-light in the town; the tax collectors begin to make their appearance; the Sisters of Mercy set up school and the Crimean war breaks out in November.

There are bitter complaints about the tax collectors......'and to add to the bliss of Ireland we have added to an already numerous staff of blood-suckers — the income-tax collectors.'

On Christmas Day a hurricane swept across the country and the bad weather continued.

'We have nothing but continual rain and sleet with occasional claps of thunder and vivid flashes of lightning.'

In early January a large number of ejectment processes came before the courts. The land is to be cleared of people, the small fields made into large ones and cattle and sheep set to graze where once people flourished. We can see the effect of this legal process in January.

'To the parish of Addergool the relieving officer was summoned. Hundreds of poor wretches, men, women and children, the sick and the dying, were cast out into the open air regardless of the cold and wet, and their dwellings — those cabins endeared to them by many happy reminiscences - pulled down before them by a posse of Barbarians. Those poor peasants who never closed their doors against the poor and needy in a short space of time saw themselves without a roof or shelter.'

Frederick Cavendish continued to rail against the injustice of the landlords and already he is sowing the seeds of opposition to the land system in farmers minds. Later James Daly would take up the challenge. It is not by chance that the Land League was set up in Mayo.

At the beginning of February there is great excitement when Mr. Thomas Brennan switches on gas lights in his shop.

'Within the past week crowds of admiring people have been attracted to the shop windows of our enterprising townsman, Mr. Thomas Brennan, to witness the strange phenomenon in Mayo of gas-lights. What renders the circumstance of such light more surprising here is the fact that Mr. Brennan unaided by any person conversant with the fixing of gasometers, has succeeded in making the gas. He has also made the required fixtures and in doing all this his secret was kept a hidden mystery to all beyond the precincts of his domestic circle until the magic spell was broken by the sudden refulgent blaze of gas, like brilliant stars, dimming the candlelight in the adjoining shops.

'The question now arises; what is to hinder the people of Castlebar, Ballina and Westport entering into an arrangement with their enterprising countyman for lighting their shops and houses. Years ago he sculpted in wood and stone and then he turned to hydraulics, by means of which he has supplied the rooms of his large establishment with hot and cold water....and this without the aid of a plumber.'

This hardware merchant was the father of Louis Philip Brennan, the inventor of the dirigible torpedo and the gyroscopic monorail. Another son Michael (1839-1871) worked as a journalist with the Connaught Telegraph. He was a talented caricaturist in his youth. Later he became quite famous as an artist and two of his paintings are in the national Gallery of Ireland. He died in Algeria and is buried there. Thomas Brennan and his wife would sell their business in 1861 and emigrate to Australia.

Gold seems to turn up regularly.

'The fact of the existence of gold in the soil of Mayo was perfectly established last week in the yard of Mr. Brennan's where his workmen were sinking a hole for the erection of his gasometer. The ore found has been tested by Dr. Atkinson who pronounced it to be pure gold.'

With the arrival of April the flow of emigration widens.

'Within the past week several persons from this town and neighbourhood have taken their departure hence for Liverpool en route to the United States. Among them were many young females, for some of whom the passage money was paid by brothers and sisters who had previously emigrated.'

Here the emigrant trails are set down for Mayo people. The American connection is built up and America beckons.

The sight of people walking with children on

their backs on the long distance to Dublin brings this remark about the workhouse.

'We have in the poorhouse young women and girls, tumbling in fat, reared up in idle habits like exotics in a hot-house, and boys trained up in idleness and engendering the most depraved habits.'

In June a better-class emigrant leaves the town judging by the luxury of departure.

'On Monday morning last the green in front of the coach-office in the town was densely crowded with weeping parents, relatives and neighbours taking a long (perhaps last) farewell of no less than nineteen male and female emigrants going by Bianconi's car to Athenry and thence to Liverpool en route to America.'

This was a pattern which would continue when the railway station was built in Castlebar. The same scenes would be witnessed for over a hundred years. The railway stations would become our wailing walls, as mothers watch the final carriage of the train turn the northern corner and disappear. But at least the hunger was behind them and they had recovered from the famine.

In June twenty persons from the barony of Murrisk marched through the town. The majority of them were pauper boys dressed in new suits of fustian with which they had been supplied by Westport guardians.'

With the deepening of the river the wells had gone dry...."and the children of the town can now almost play hop-scotch or marbles on the bed of the newly-constructed river. As for the millers we fancy they must turn their grinding establishments into windmills.'

A system of education seems to have established itself in the workhouse. The master tailor states that he sent out fourteen boys who had established themselves about the country. Others were learning their trade in the weaver's shop.

In June the Sisters of Mercy arrived in the town. 'For many years we have been hearing complaints, and justly so, for the want of a respectable seminary for the education of young ladies. That want is at length happily supplied by the Sisters of Mercy, who have established a branch of their blessed institution in this town and have opened a school.'

The Sisters of Mercy extend their ministry to the workhouse. A resolution was passed by the board 'that the Sisters of Mercy be admitted to visit and give religious instruction to the Roman Catholic patients in the infirmary and fever hospital and that they also be permitted to visit the male and female schools and give religious instruction there to Roman Catholic children at the hour set apart each day in the week for religious instruction.'

There would be continued tension between members of the board and the Sisters of Mercy during the coming year.

The religious troubles of the day can be seen in the following announcement..'We are enabled to inform our readers that a young man named Heveran, for some time teaching school in Rehins for Mr. Stoney, and who ranked as one of the proselytes fished up in this neighbourhood, got tired of the humbug system as he designated it and sent last week to His Grace the Archbishop for, and obtained , pardon for the scandal he brought to the church, and he is once more a rigid and uncompromising member of the flock of Christ.'

It is a year of development. Not only is gas-lighting now possible, it is announced that 'with submarine telegraph which is about to be laid down between the new world and Galway that Great Britain and America will be come one colossal country.'

In August the army went in search of recruits.

'On Saturday last a number of sergeants and privates of the 16th Depot quartered in Castlebar beat up through the town for recruits and although they played all the tunes best calculated to rouse the ears of Irishmen they didn't succeed in getting one recruit. It would appear that our youngsters are getting as wary as old rooks and they have no desire of being made into soup by either Russian or Kafir soldiers.'

There was joy for one old man in the town when entered the shop of Henry Murphy to beg for a bit of tobacco. To his surprise a cheque had arrived from his son in Brooklyn for 4 pounds..and more was promised.

While all the small events of the town are happening the Crimean War ripens. It will be remembered most for the charge of the Light Brigade and Lord Cardigan and Lord Lucan will become bitter enemies when it is finished.

But now the town is seized with three panics. The first panic is for food. The blight has returned.

Secondly there are rumours from Europe that cholera is devastating that vast continent. 'Merciful God we invoke Thee to stay the career of this terrible epidemic' The third panic is the panic caused from sewers choked by stagnant and putrid waters and the effluvia rising on high from filthy yards and archways and the diseased beef on the streets.

There is no water to wash through the new bed of the river which has been deepened too much and cannot take the sewage from the military barracks. An inscription is suggested for the new bridge;

"This river was lowered to draw the water, And this Jews Harp was built to keep the water from flowing and to collect the scourings of sewers and other filthy reservoirs — A. D. 1853."

Although there is a general wish to bring the railroad west through Castlebar, the dangers of travelling by rail are expressed in the following report:

'On Wednesday last on the railroad from Killarney to Dublin there was an accident by which 14 human beings were hurried into the presence of their God and many others so shockingly mangled as to leave but little hope for their recovery and even should they survive must remain maimed for life.'

In October a lady who has made a voyage on the Amanda under Captain Cromwell assures her friends in Castlebar by letter that the voyage was entirely satisfactory. Mr. Miller, the Government agent in Westport, was so strict a disciplinarian that he would not permit a vessel to clear the port unless she was in the most perfect order.

In late October there is witnessed in Castlebar a ceremony, the first of its kind since the Reformation. Two nuns were professed, one the daughter of a patriotic townsman called H. Murphy.

In November war between Russia and Turkey is finally declared. This is of a more local nature than it's remoteness might suggest. Lord Lucan would voyage to the Crimea. He would fall into bad favour with the British public over the famous Charge of the Light Brigade, an event which would bring Cecil Woodham-Smith to Castlebar and inspire her to write 'The Great Hunger.'

While there was news concerning the outbreak of the Crimean War, it is also reported that Mr. William Devine, a respectable tradesman of the town, died of lockjaw occasioned by a nail having entered the ball of his big toe through his shoe.

In late November two urchins are taken into custody.

'Although young in years they are old in vice. They robbed a country woman of her shoes which she was in the act of putting on her feet at the Shambles Bridge in this town. They were sent to jail and sentenced to three months each and to be once whipped. These young scions are from that villainous den of iniquity, Gallows Hill.'

December was not a very cheerful month. The price of bread doubled and the price of potatoes and meal followed. The poor labourers are seen standing in the street shivering in the cold winter blast not having a turn to do.

But there was promise of goodly fare at the Workhouse.

'We understand that through the kindness of Very Rev. Archdeacon MacHale, the Roman Catholic Chaplain, the Rev. W. B. Stoney, Protestant Chaplain, and Doctor Barrett, Medical Superintendent, the paupers of the poor house will be supplied with meat on Christmas Day. May God reward those who comfort the poor thus.'

The town of Castlebar has come through the terrible years. It has passed through famine and eviction. This memory, carried to America and England, is lodged in the consciousness of Mayo people to this very day. One child was born during the famine who would change the possession of land in Ireland forever. His name was Michael Davitt and he was born in Straide on 25th of March 1846. When he was four years of age his family was evicted from their holding during the great clearances. He will become the father of the Land League. He is Mayo's most famous son and he comes out of these terrible times.

All this is in the future. Gas-light illuminates the streets of Castlebar. This is the light of hope.